AMC guide to

Country Walks Near MONTREAL

within reach by
public transportation

by William G. Scheller
Photographs by Paul Mozell
Mapwork by Robert Holloran

COUNTRY WALKS NEAR MONTREAL

Copyright © 1982 by William G. Scheller
All rights reserved.
Printed in the United States of America.
No part of this book may be used or reproduced in any manner
whatsoever without written permission except in the case of brief
quotations embodied in critical articles and reviews.
If you find any errors in the text or maps, or can suggest
improvements, you are urged to send a letter to the Appalachian
Mountain Club, attention Country Walks, 5 Joy Street, Boston,
Massachusetts 02108.

FIRST EDITION

ISBN 0-910146-40-3

To the Dilas of Westmount —
Kay, Michael, John, and Mary

CONTENTS

Foreword   1

Introduction   4

1/ Mount Royal Park   6
Walking and ski touring — a walk of approximately 2 miles, with side-trail possibilities, within a mountaintop park at the center of Montreal. Excellent views of the city and its environs, along with visits to a grand chalet and a 100-foot steel cross.

2/ Oka — Paul Sauve Park   16
Walking, ski touring, and snowshoeing — 27 miles of trails in a provincial park on the Lake of Two Mountains. Hiking in the Oak Hills, along an old pilgrimage route, with a side trip to an historic monastery.

3/ Mount St. Bruno   24
Walking, ski touring, and snowshoeing — 6 miles of trail (more in winter) circling lakes and crisscrossing a mature upland forest in a hilltop provincial park. An historic stone mill, and a picnic area set amidst an apple orchard.

4/ Cape St. Jacques   32
Walking, ski touring, and snowshoeing — woods, meadows, and scenic coastline in a new 690-acre peninsular park maintained by the Urban Community of Montreal (CUM).

5/ Morgan Arboretum   40
Walking and ski touring — 12 miles of trails in a 600-acre arboretum near the western tip of Montreal Island. Tree species from throughout Canada grow here, in environments ranging from pocket wilderness to managed plantations.

6/ Longueuil Outdoor Center/City of Longueuil   **48**
Walking, ski touring, cycling, and a variety of other outdoor activities on a new 450-acre preserve, with 10 miles of trails, just across the St. Lawrence from Montreal. Later, a walk through the older precincts of Longueuil, where a number of historic buildings have been preserved.

7/ Parc Angrignon-Lachine Canal   **58**
Ski touring, bicycling, and walking — 4¾ miles, each direction. Beginning at Angrignon Park, the ski touring route continues along an historic canal to the city of Lachine, once the eastern terminus of the fur trade.

8/ Maisonneuve Park/ Montreal Botanical Garden   **68**
Walking — ski touring in winter in Maisonneuve Park, adjacent to Botanical Garden grounds. During growing season, a beautifully varied outdoor display of trees, shrubs, flowers, herbs, ornamentals, and other plants; also, extensive indoor displays throughout the year.

9/ Ile des Moulins — Terrebonne   **76**
Walking — 1 mile on island; also walks in the adjoining town of Terrebonne. A restoration of the office and mills belonging to an historic seigneurial estate on the Riviere des Mille Iles.

10/ Mount St. Hilaire Nature Conservation Center   **86**
Walking, ski touring, and snowshoeing — 15 miles of trails traversing a 1,500-acre preserve on Mt. St. Hilaire, one of the Monteregian hills that rises to the east of Montreal. Despite hundreds of years of settlement on the surrounding plain, the center's property has remained a virtual wilderness.

11/ Cote St. Catherine Park/St. Lawrence Seaway   **94**
Walking and cycling — a park on the south shore of the St. Lawrence River, separated from the mainland by the St. Lawrence Seaway. From the park, an 8½-mile

bicycle path extends along the Seaway to Nun's Island and the Victoria Bridge.

12/ Rigaud   104
Walking and ski touring, with a 1½-mile trail linking the Shrine of Our Lady of Lourdes, the geologically fascinating "Devil's Garden," and the summit of Rigaud Mountain.

13/ Iles de Boucherville Provincial Park   112
Walking and bicycling — 4-1/2 miles of foot and bike trails on Ile Ste. Marguerite, with footbridges and further trail development planned for four other islands. A provincial park surrounded by water, just north of downtown Montreal, the Iles de Boucherville have remained largely obscure since their days as part of a land grant to one of the old seigneurs of New France.

14/ Angrignon Park — Aqueduct Canal — Lachine Rapids   122
Walking, ski touring, and bicycling — 7 miles (slightly longer from Metro). A new path follows Montreal's Aqueduct Canal into the town of Lasalle, where it empties into the St. Lawrence just above the Lachine Rapids. Return along the river, with a close-up view of the rapids.

15/ Ile de la Visitation/Riviere des Prairies/Boise Heritage   130
A trip to the northern and eastern reaches of the island of Montreal, where we find three parks-in-the-making which will considerably expand the horizons of area walkers, ski tourers, and cyclists.

16/ Les Forestiers Outdoor Center   142
Walking, ski touring, and snowshoeing — 10 miles of trails in a unique 1200-acre outdoor recreation and education center 30 miles west of Montreal on the peninsula which lies between the Lake of Two Mountains and the St. Lawrence River. Camping and lodge accommodations are available for overnight visitors; special attention is given to school groups.

FOREWORD

MOST GUIDES FOR THE FOOT TRAVELER are concerned either with city streets or backwoods trails. This book, the fourth in the Appalachian Mountain Club's *Country Walks* series, is about the world which lies between these two extremes. Its sixteen chapters suggest walks that can easily be incorporated into trips of a single day's duration, but which still offer a welcome diversion from more familiar urban and suburban landscapes. Some are, truly, "country" walks; a few thread through the quieter, lesser-known corners of the city itself.

Most of the places described in *Country Walks* are accessible by public transportation. Specific directions for bus, Metro, or rail travel are given in each chapter, as are directions for driving. In all cases, downtown Montreal is assumed to be the point of departure, although connections with outlying areas may be plotted with the use of road or public transit maps. Maps of the city and its surroundings may be obtained at the information center operated by the Quebec Ministry of Tourism at 2 Place Ville Marie, downtown Montreal (514-873-2015). For detailed topographic maps, visit Conexfor Inc., in the shopping center at at Complex Desjardins on Dorchester Boulevard in downtown Montreal (514-849-5741).

Montreal's well-integrated transportation network combines both public and private services. Most important are the bus and underground "Metro" lines operated by the Transportation

COUNTRY WALKS

Commission of the Urban Community of Montreal. (The Metro, which is still expanding, is regarded as one of the cleanest, quietest, and most efficient subway systems in the world.) Joining with this extensive service are Transport de Laval, operating bus routes in the towns of Ile Jesus, north of Montreal Island; its counterpart, Metropolitan Sud, which runs the buses on the south shore of the St. Lawrence; Voyageurs, the long-distance motor coach firm; and, CP Rail. Here are the numbers to call for information concerning these major carriers:

Metro and Montreal Buses	Dial "A-U-T-O-B-U-S"
Transport de Laval	688-6520
Metropolitan Sud	676-0376
Voyageurs	842-2281
CP Rail	866-6896

The area code for all of the above numbers is 514.

Determining that public transportation serves a certain point is only part of a walker's planning. It won't do to arrive at an outlying destination, spend the day, and then learn that the last bus or train has left. Always ask about service in both directions, and check again if you plan the same walk during a different season. Every effort has been made to provide accurate information in this book, but transit schedules do change. As of this writing, a major reorganization of Montreal's regional public transportation network is being discussed, and readers are advised to keep track of new developments.

Many of the distances which can be covered in these walks are variable; often, the same area can offer a two-mile stroll or a ten-mile hike. Decide in advance how long you plan to be on the trail, so that you can work out transportation arrangements as well as lunch and clothing requirements. Most people walk at a pace of between two and three miles an hour; since the trips in this book are intended for recreation rather than rigor, the slower rate will most likely apply. Remember that snowshoeing or walking in snow can take up to twice as long as a walk of the

FOREWORD

same length on dry ground. Conversely, cross-country skiers can often put distances behind them much more quickly than pedestrians.

Check weather forecasts before you leave for a walk, and dress appropriately. Although stories of Montreal's winter weather are frequently exaggerated, it can get very cold. Sweaters and light jackets are handy even in early fall and late spring. Regardless of the season, wear sturdy, comfortable shoes or boots.

Always keep to established trails. At first, this admonition may seem to apply only to the pristine backwoods, but a minute's reflection should serve to convince walkers that open lands near large cities are every bit as fragile as the wilderness, and sometimes more so. Heavy use of these places can only be sustained if everyone treats them gently and stays on trail.

I would like to thank everyone who helped with the research for this book, especially Rolland Cousineau, Alice Johannsen, Jean Hubert, Robert Madden, Luc Morel, Jean Chaput, Professor James D. MacArthur, Father Albert Desroches, Pierre Bourque, Gabriel Ducharme, and Pierre Belec. M. Belec represents the Federation Quebecois du Plein Air, which is a valuable source of information on outdoor activities in the province.

My special thanks also go to Alice Scheller for typing the manuscript, to Paul Mozell and John Dila for the photographs, to Bob Holloran for the maps, and to Arlyn Powell, Michael Cirone, and Betsey Tryon of the Appalachian Mountain Club for editing and design of the book.

INTRODUCTION

TEN YEARS AGO, this would have been a very different book, or perhaps a much shorter one. Look at the table of contents, and you will find barely a half-dozen places that could have been included in a similar list at the beginning of the 1970's. The others are evidence of a new realization — by municipal, provincial, and federal authorities, as well as by the people of greater Montreal — of the need for preserving green spaces and providing lands for public recreation. For this we should be thankful, but along with appreciation comes the question: what took so long?

Two years ago, I spent several months traveling around the New York area to collect material for another volume in this series. Despite the size of that city, and the fact that its metropolitan shadow stretches much farther than Montreal's, I found an abundance of parks, reserves, paths, and trails. What was most surprising, though, was the fact that many of these natural treasures had been accessible — had been protected either by public consensus or official sanction — for the better part of a century. If this was the case on the doorstep of New York, a city whose appetite for land is a thing terrible to behold, how should we explain Montreal, which appears to have caught up only recently with its citizens' need to stretch their legs?

The answer surely doesn't lie with an indifference to the land. "Though many things have changed for the Quebecois in this century," writes Joel Garreau in his book *The Nine Nations of North America*, "the acres of Quebec, its river and mountains and towns, are still integral to their nationalism." Yes — but there can be a difference between loving the land, and taking deliberate steps to husband certain parcels of it, between a vague affinity for *mon pays* and the perception that open, accessible country is in peril.

If Montreal has lagged behind New York in the development of a preservationist ethic, it is likely because it had far more time to take its land for granted. To most people living in southern Quebec before the middle of the twentieth century, worrying about setting aside open land would have been comparable to lobbying for the conservation of muskeg in the Yukon. Montreal was an island, but in more ways than one. The vastness of the St. Lawrence lowlands, and of the forests which still cover the Canadian Shield to the north, must have made the supply of open vistas seem endless. New York felt that way too at one time, but there the realization came sooner that while the numbers of people, buildings, and automobiles were increasing, the number of acres was not.

Happily, that same awareness has come to Montreal. There is evidence of it not only along the far outskirts, but throughout the island city, where expansive new parks are being sited on land that might once have been consigned to tract houses and shopping malls. And, in the construction of bikeways, and of paths for skiers and pedestrians, Montreal has far surpassed New York. You can ski the length of the Lachine Canal, or cycle along the St. Lawrence Seaway. There's nothing like that in Manhattan, unless you count the old West Side Highway — and that's being torn down to make room for a new Interstate.

So, it's better to come around late than not at all, and Montreal has more than made up for lost time. Enjoy the new parks and trails in this corner of Quebec, along with traditional retreats such as Mt. Royal, Maisonneuve Park, and the mountain at Rigaud. The acres of Quebec are integral not only to nationalism, but to the health and good spirits of its natives and visitors alike.

1

MOUNT ROYAL PARK

Walking and ski touring — a walk of approximately 2 miles, with side-trail possibilities, within a mountaintop park at the center of Montreal. Excellent views of the city and its environs, along with visits to a grand chalet and a 100-foot steel cross.

THERE MUST HAVE BEEN TIMES, when Frederick Law Olmsted was working on the plans for Mount Royal Park, when he wished he had gone into another line of work.

It is one thing to cope with trees, with rocks, with the grading of roads and meadows; this is the landscape architect's stock in trade. It is quite another matter, though, to deal with politicians, and with a public that does not understand genius. Olmsted's commission to design Mount Royal caused him no end of headaches, and he set down a record of the whole nettlesome business in an 1881 monograph that amounts as much to an *apologia* for his style of landscaping as it does a record of the project.

Olmsted wasn't eager to take the job in the first place. In order to do justice to "so unusual a problem," he felt that he should have lived for a while near the site, so that he might become familiar with its natural advantages and limitations. This was no small consideration. Olmsted was adamant in his belief that landscape design should evolve from the possibilities inherent in a place — so much so that he urged that the term "park" not even be used to describe the Mount Royal property. "Park," to

Olmsted, implied the whole array of artificial impositions with which nineteenth-century developers sought to improve, but only succeeded in cluttering and degrading, open spaces set aside for public recreation. Olmsted was not a man for pavilions, amusements, bandstands, and skating rinks heaped upon one another: one or two of such things might be alright in their place, but for a spot such as Mount Royal, nature — and a gentle, almost imperceptible accommodation with it — was everything. Montreal, he wrote, had opportunities for a public park which no other city enjoyed, and it would be a "scandalous extravagance" to waste them. Here, according to Olmsted, there was "an element of value much more important...than inducements to take air and exercise — the *intrinsic* value of charming natural scenery" (italics his).

Easily said. But getting Montreal officialdom to go along with this then-radical theory of park design was a different story. The City Council would come up with one set of objections, their appointed park commissioners another. The Council wanted to push a bridle road straight through a picnic ground; the commissioners — and Olmsted — did not. Sides were drawn along similar lines when other issues came up, although the architect occasionally complained that the commissioners were forced to betray their own better judgment by uninformed, "popular" pressure. Virtually all Montreal wanted a park on the mountain, but few people could agree on what it should look like.

It took Olmsted three years to submit the final draft of his plan for Mount Royal Park. When it was completed, he was told that the City Council was likely to change its mind regarding some of the premises the plan was based on. The politicians had been changing their minds, making and unmaking decisions, since Olmsted first came north to take on the project; now, he had finished his plan "only to find that it must be thrown up and the work begun anew at the bottom." Exasperation: "We, who are to pay the bills," the Council told the American, "have an interest in economy, you know." But Olmsted pointed out that had his advice not been constantly overruled — had his natural-

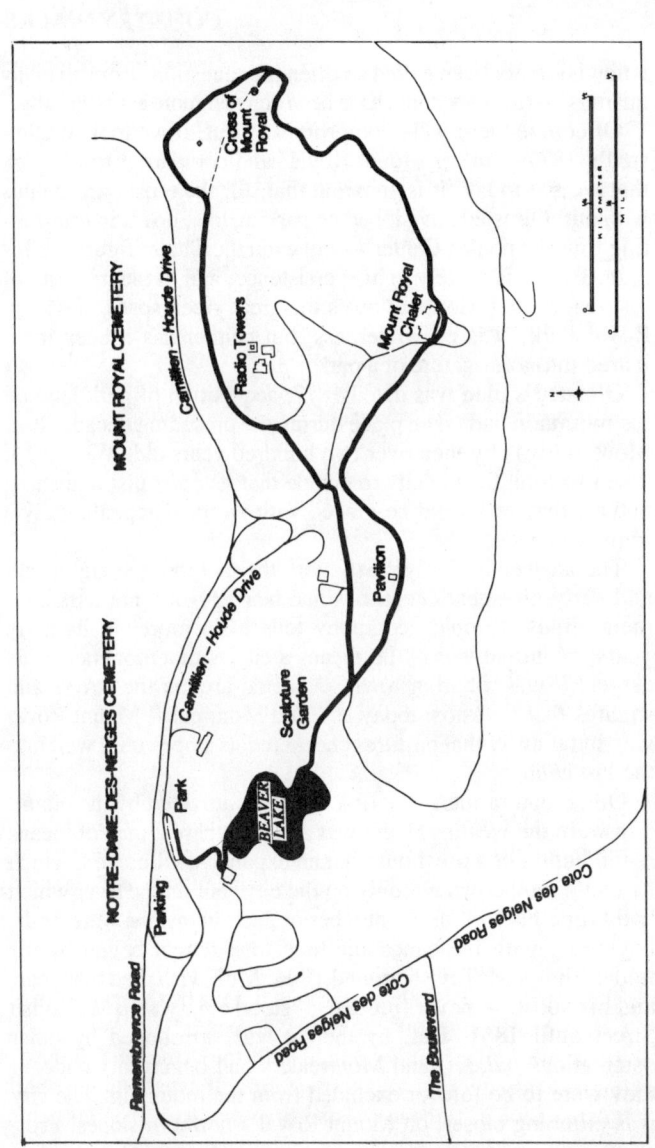

COUNTRY WALKS

istic vision not been called so often into question, from so many quarters — the work could have been done far more economically.

Of course there were compromises. But, if we look at Olmsted's 1877 plan for Mount Royal, and compare it to the park that we see today, it is apparent that, for the most part, genius won out. Olmsted envisioned no parking lots, no radio transmitting towers, no Art Center — not even the Chalet figured in his plan. But, it is largely to his persistence, and to the integrity of his vision, that Montreal owes the great green space of Mount Royal Park. It is no wilderness, but neither has it been manicured into a caricature of a park.

Olmsted's plan was dated 1877; acquisition of park land on the mountain had taken place during the preceding decade. But, Montreal was by then over two hundred years old. Why had it taken so long for the city to decide that its most distinguishing natural feature should be graced with its most appealing civic improvement?

The answer lies only partly with the fact that the eighteenth and early nineteenth centuries had beaver pelts, not parks, on their minds. Simple geography tells even more: in its early years, Montreal was by no means a city with a mountain at its center. It was a harbor town, clustered around the streets and squares that we know today as "Old Montreal." Mount Royal was so far away that pastures checkered its slopes until well into the last century.

Other than farmers, the first residents attracted by the mountain were the wealthy. Here was a place where a man of means could build not a row house but an expansive villa, from which he could look down not only on the city, but on the river which had borne his fortune. A number of such mansions were built, beginning with the handsome limestone retreat begun by fur trader Simon McTavish around 1804. McTavish died that year, and his house — never finished — stood empty atop McTavish Street until 1861. But, by then it was surrounded by other ostentatious *palazzi,* and Montrealers had begun to wonder if they were to be forever excluded from the mountain. The city was climbing closer; on Mount Royal's northern slopes, Prot-

MOUNT ROYAL PARK

estant and Catholic cemeteries had already been established. Farsighted citizens realized that acquisition of land for a park must begin.

All this, needless to say, is recent history by Montreal standards. And, it is ironic — though in the light of the early settlement's embracing of the river, understandable — that the city's "discovery" of the mountain should have occurred so late. For Mount Royal figures in the account of the very first visit by Europeans to the Island of Montreal, and it was on the occasion of that visit that Jacques Cartier gave the mountain the name which it came to share with the city. Cartier climbed Mount Royal with members of his party and his Indian hosts on an October day in 1535. The Indians lived in the village of Hochelaga, which is believed to have been located near the present-day campus of McGill University, on Sherbrooke Street. No doubt the Hochelagans wished to show Cartier the view. It is just as spectacular today, though vastly altered by the cleverness and hydro fire of Cartier's race.

PUBLIC TRANSIT: If you are already in downtown Montreal, transportation to Mount Royal Park is a simple matter. The downtown stops along Metro Line 1 put you within easy reach of the park by bus or foot, although you should remember that from Boulevard Maisonneuve, where the Metro stations are located, it is uphill all the way. For the walk outlined below, you can get off at Guy station and take any of the buses (as of this writing, Numbers 65, 66, and 165) that head north on Cote des Neiges Road. Ask the driver to let you off at the park entrance, which is a right turn at the beginning of Camillien-Houde Drive. From the Mount Royal station on Metro Line 2, take the Number 11 bus, which follows Camillien-Houde Drive through the park.

AUTOMOBILE: The main automobile approaches to Mount Royal Park are Park Avenue, on the east, and Cote

COUNTRY WALKS

des Neiges Road, on the west. Camillien-Houde Drive connects the two, separating the north slopes of the mountain from the cemeteries of Mount Royal (Protestant) and Notre Dame des Neiges (Catholic). For this walk, take Cote des Neiges north to the park entrance (see above) and park at the metered lot adjoining the Beaver Lake pavilion.

As you approach Mount Royal Park from the west, you will notice that Cote des Neiges Road follows a depression between two summits. Mount Royal itself is on the right; on the left is Westmount, which gives the surrounding community its name. This declivity between the two summits makes Mount Royal into something of a "double" mountain, although a geological dissimilarity must be noted. Mount Royal, at 759 feet, is one of the smallest of the eight Monteregian Hills that dot this corner of Quebec. Like the others, it is composed of a solidified intrusion of igneous material exposed by the elements over a vast amount of time. (It is not, as is commonly supposed, an extinct volcano.) The Westmount summit, however, is made up largely of sedimentary rock.

There is a park at the Westmount summit, with parking available at several locations along Summit Circle. Although much smaller than Mount Royal, this is a pleasant place for short walks and cross-country skiing.

A third, man-made summit dominates this part of Montreal, actually achieving a height which surpasses that of Mount Royal by 97 feet. This is the dome of St. Joseph's Oratory, visible to the north and west just off Cote des Neiges Road. It is second in size only to that of St. Peter's in Rome, and crowns an enormous basilica built between 1924 and 1966, largely through the efforts of the remarkable Brother Andre. The Oratory, which is open daily, has become a revered shrine. Depending upon one's faith, its fascination can be either religious or cultural — but in any event, it is well worth a visit.

THE WALK: Beginning at the parking lot near the Cote des Neige entrance to Mount Royal Park, walk uphill past the

COUNTRY WALKS

sculpture garden, with Beaver Lake on your right. Follow the gravel path, crossing one road before you reach the crest of the hill. After a short distance, you will come to a small open pavilion on your left; just past this point, on your right, a network of dirt paths leads off into the glades and thickets of the mountain's south slope. There are places along these paths where you can adjust your field of vision to include nothing but trees and sky — it isn't hard to imagine yourself far from the gates of Montreal, alert for signs of an Iroquois ambush. You won't get lost; just follow any of the paths uphill to rejoin the main trail.

Continue for less than ½ mile to reach Mount Royal Chalet. The Chalet is built along the lines of a seigneurial hall, and the beams of its buttressed ceiling are highlighted with the royal blue of old France. Above its windows on the interior walls is a series of 17 murals depicting famous moments in the history of Montreal, and above the fireplace are the coats of arms of Champlain, Cartier, Maisonneuve, Canada, Great Britain, and the *ancien regime* of France.

The terrace outside the Chalet affords a fine view of the city, suburbs, and river. On especially clear days, you can see as far as the mountains of northern Vermont. Bronze arrows set in the railing of the terrace point out the sights in the city and along the horizon.

Facing the Chalet from the terrace, turn to the right and follow the gravel trail towards the eastern end of the mountain. (Don't take the sharp right leading down the slope, nor the smaller path to the left of the main trail which leads directly uphill.) After ½ to ¾ mile, you will reach the Cross of Mount Royal, an illuminated steel structure erected in 1924.

This cross is not the first to stand atop the mountain. Late in 1642, the St. Lawrence flooded its banks, threatening the new settlement of Ville Marie. The waters receded on Christmas

MOUNT ROYAL PARK

Day, and on January 6 — the feast of the Epiphany — a grateful Sieur de Maisonneuve carried a makeshift cross up a freshly-blazed trail, and set it near this spot.

From the cross, follow the gravel road around to the north slope of the mountain, or bear right along the dirt paths that lead from behind the cross and join the road after it loops back towards the west. As you return to Beaver Lake, the transmitting towers of Radio Canada and the dome of St. Joseph's Oratory stand directly ahead, while to the right are the two cemeteries and the tower of the University of Montreal. The gravel road here parallels Camillien-Houde Road, along which the Number 11 bus runs.

After passing the radio towers, the road curves to the left. When you reach the point at which the first broad view of the river appears (the towers are now almost directly to your left), look for a dirt path leading downhill. Follow this path, keeping to the left where it forks, and you will reach a parking lot. Follow the paved road, with the parking lot to your right, to return to the sculpture garden and Beaver Lake.

2

OKA-PAUL SAUVE PARK

Walking, ski touring, and snowshoeing — 27 miles of trails in a provincial park on the Lake of Two Mountains. Hiking in the Oka Hills, along an old pilgrimage route, with a side trip to an historic monastery.

TO THOUSANDS OF PEOPLE throughout North America, the name "Oka" conjures up an image of bright orange-and-blue wrapping around a gouda-shaped cheese. Semisoft and subtle in flavor, Oka cheese is made by Trappist monks of the monastery of La Trappe, just outside the town of Oka and within two miles of Paul Sauve Provincial Park. It is about as benign an export as a place can have, especially considering its manufacture by a community of brothers not even given to conversation, let alone controversy. But there was a time in Quebec's history when mention of Oka quickened tempers rather than palates. It was a different religious fraternity, the Sulpicians, who were at the center of the storm.

The Gentlemen of St. Sulpice were founded about the same time as Montreal. The purpose envisioned by their organizer, Abbe Jacques Olier, was in fact the conversion of the Indian tribes of the upper St. Lawrence. By 1666, King Louis XIV had confirmed the Sulpicians as seigneurs of the Island of Montreal, thus giving them impressive temporal as well as spiritual powers. Their mission among the natives continued, and in 1676 they founded a settlement for Christian Indians on the slopes of Mount Royal.

COUNTRY WALKS

In 1717, the Sulpicians removed their mission to Oka, where they had been granted another seigneurial title. There the priests administered and evangelized, and the Indians lived and worked, without much notice during the following 150 years. By the 1860's, though, conditions at the mission had deteriorated, and the world outside had changed. Trouble was brewing at Oka.

By that time, Quebec had been in British hands for a hundred years, although the tangle of old seigneurial claims — particularly those involving Catholic Church holdings — had not been systematically undone. The Sulpicians were still masters of their little domain at Oka. But, with the British had come Protestantism, and by the middle of the nineteenth century Catholic priests were not the only ones proselytizing among the natives. The Methodists, in particular, were active around Oka, where they were able to make significant inroads among a population of Iroquois, Algonquins, and Nipissings whose material condition — according to Protestant accounts — left much to be desired. "Poor and oppressed" were the words used by Rev. John Borland, a Protestant writer of the period, to describe the Indians; elsewhere, he cites instances of their being harassed and even arrested for cutting wood on what Borland felt was their own land. Also, there was the matter of farms being let out by the priests to white French Canadians.

The ultimate confrontation, though, came when some of the Indians decided to build a Methodist church on the grounds of the seigneury. According to Borland, at least three-quarters of the settlement's population had converted to Wesleyan Methodism by 1868, and in 1871 they proposed the construction of a Protestant place of worship. The Sulpicians would have none of it; in fact, they tore down a small church structure as soon as the Indians put it up. At issue was the proper ownership of the land. The Sulpicians argued that legal title was given them by the royal grant and the British government's subsequent confirmation — in the Act of 1840 — of all such grants which had not been nullified at the time of New France's capitulation. The Protestants took the position that the Act did no more than to

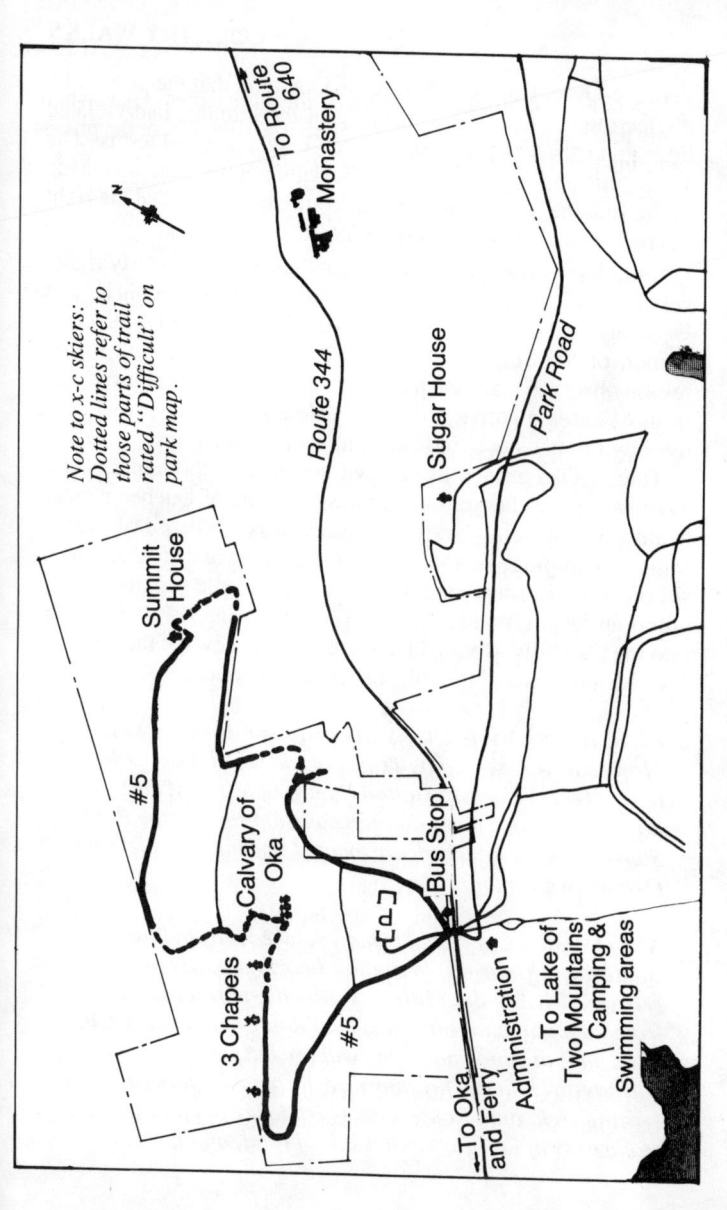

COUNTRY WALKS

give the Order trusteeship over the land, and that the priests, by neglecting the material well-being of the Indians, had violated both this trusteeship and the French king's original terms. The 1717 petition for the seigneury, Borland pointed out, was made in the Indians' name. How, then, could they be denied the right to erect whatever sort of church they chose?

It all came down to the Sulpicians' claims of property rights versus the Protestants' charge that the Indians were being held in vassalage and denied freedom of worship. Eventually, the Gentlemen of St. Sulpice had to yield; a 1905 guidebook to the region observes that "each hamlet now has its little church, and in most cases a native preacher." Note the word "preacher," used by Protestants to indicate a minister, not a priest.

Today, Oka enjoys its renown not only as the home of the Trappists' fine cheese, but as the site of one of Quebec's most beautiful provincial parks. Paul Sauve has a little bit of everything — camping, swimming, fishing, hiking and cross-country ski trails, three snowshoeing areas, and a maple sugarhouse — all on an ideal lakeside setting. The hiking and ski trails climb into the Oka hills, from which there are fine views of the Lake of Two Mountains and the surrounding countryside.

PUBLIC TRANSIT: Oka is situated some 30 miles west of Montreal. It is served by Transport de Laval buses, which leave Henri Bourassa station (Metro Line 2, last northbound stop) four times daily. Buses stop right at the Paul Sauve Park gates, which are located just under a mile from Oka's town center.

AUTOMOBILE: From downtown, take Metropolitan Boulevard (Route 40) to Route 13 north. Shortly after crossing Riviere des Mille Iles, which separates Laval from the mainland, turn west onto Route 640. Follow 640 to its end, at which point you will see the park signs. Here you have a choice of heading directly onto the park road or turning right onto Route 344, which takes you past the monastery of La Trappe (left side of road) and joins the

OKA-PAUL SAUVE PARK

park road at its western terminus, which is where the walk described below begins.

Motorists have a pleasant option for their return trip. During ice-free months, a ferry crosses the Lake of Two Mountains between the town of Oka and Como, on the lake's south shore. Less than a mile west of the Como landing is the Willow Inn, a cheery spot dispensing port, stilton, and steak and kidney pie. To return to Montreal from Como, head east on the shore road to join Route 40, the Trans Canada Highway.

THE WALK: Obtain a map of Paul Sauve Park at the entrance, near the intersection of the park road and Route 344. Be sure to get the winter map which outlines six separate cross-country ski trails, most of which are equally suitable for hiking (Trail 6 leads through the lakeside camping areas and alongside the swimming beaches, which are not places in which to seek solitude in summer). Perhaps the best hiking route is the one which leads uphill from the parking area on the right (inland) side of Route 344, and which is marked Number 5 on the park map and on the map accompanying this chapter.

Following these maps, you will be able to make a circuit — on foot or on skis — of the higher elevations of Paul Sauve Park. If you're skiing cross-country, be sure to take note that certain sections of the trail are rated "difficult." The remainder of the route shown is rated "medium."

Along one section of the trail (see symbols on map), you will come upon a series of tiny, whitewashed chapels, culminating in a hilltop formation of three simple structures known as the "Calvary of Oka." These wayside chapels were built by local Indians in the early 1740's under the direction of Sulpician missionaries. They served to instruct the new converts in the way of the cross, and were long an attraction to white pilgrims as well. The final three buildings are arranged to suggest the

COUNTRY WALKS

position of Christ's crucifix and those of the two thieves with whom he was put to death. The view from this point is magnificent. Since the hills are largely forested with hardwoods, early autumn is an especially good time for a hike here.

At the eastern extreme of this trail circuit stands a summit house, which serves as a warm-up shelter for skiers. Displays along the inside walls offer information (in French) about the flora and fauna of the area.

The approximate length of the Number 5 trail circuit is 4½ miles, less if the shortcut cross trails are used.

If you are driving, or if you wish to walk the two-mile distance from the park entrance, a visit to the La Trappe monastery store makes an interesting side trip. Here the Trappists sell their famous Oka cheese (note: serve at room temperature), along with many other varieties produced on and off the premises. There is also a selection of religious books and articles. The store is staffed by members of the order wearing their traditional robes. Trappists take a vow of silence; presumably, the brothers chosen to sell to the public are temporarily dispensed from this obligation.

We should not take leave of Oka without a word or two about its curious geology. The "Oka Complex," as geologists call it, consists largely of magmatic intrusions of carbonatites and other early Cretaceous materials in a series of "ring-dikes." Some 66 mineral species are found here, including two — niocalite and latrappite — that had been previously unknown to science. These Cretaceous intrusions are of an age similar to that of Mount Royal and the other Monteregian hills — about 100 million years. That was, in a manner of speaking, last week. The Precambrian "basement rocks" through which the dikes forced their way are products of Laurentian time, which came to a close some 2½ billion years ago. This is the stuff of the Laurentian Range itself, which stands to the north and constitutes the oldest mountain formation in the world. Everything is relative: think about the Laurentians, and the question of Methodists versus Sulpicians begins to loom a little less large.

OKA-PAUL SAUVE PARK

Paul Sauve Park, Oka, Quebec, is open for camping from mid-May to mid-September. Hours for snowshoeing and cross-country skiing are from 8 A.M. to 4 P.M., with trails open to hikers during the rest of the year. For information, call the Quebec Ministry of Tourism, Hunting, and Fishing at 514-873-2763, or park headquarters at 514-473-1460.

3

MOUNT ST. BRUNO

Walking, ski touring, and snowshoeing — 6 miles of trail (more in winter) circling lakes and crisscrossing a mature upland forest in a hilltop provincial park. An historic stone mill, and a picnic area set amidst an apple orchard.

WHAT MAKES A MOUNTAIN a mountain? It's all a matter of perspective. To anyone who has spent time in the Rockies or the Caucasus — or even in the Laurentians of Quebec — the idea of tacking the word "Mount" onto any of the protrusions in the Montreal area might seem patently absurd. But look again: the terrain here is so horizontal, so unrelieved by any natural features other than the St. Lawrence and its tributaries, that eight little igneous interruptions are given a lot more attention than they would otherwise deserve. These are the Monteregian Hills: Mounts Royal, St. Bruno, St. Hilaire, Johnson, Yamaska, Shefford, and Brome; and Rougemont, which has its dignity built into its name in both French and English. They take their appellation from a Latinizing of "Mount Royal," and they range eastward from Montreal along a fifty-mile axis. Of the eight, Mt. St. Bruno is one of the smallest, and it is the lowest — at barely 650 feet — in elevation.

Before looking into the formation of the Monteregian Hills, we should give some thought to why the territory around them is so flat. The answer has to do with prolonged and relatively

COUNTRY WALKS

uneventful periods of sedimentation, during an epoch in which the St. Lawrence valley was at the bottom of the sea.

We aren't talking here about the Champlain Sea, a phenomenon as recent in geological time as yesterday's drying puddles, but about a submergence of the Precambrian "basement rock" which lasted through the Cambrian, Ordovician, Silurian, and Devonian periods. This was a span of some 200 million years, throughout which assorted strata of mud and sand settled upon the floor of this vanished sea, forming the sedimentary layers which geologists are able to identify today. The earliest stratum they have discovered is a Cambrian deposit known as Potsdam sandstone (500–570 million years old), which lies over 2,000 feet beneath the surface of Montreal. Ordovician strata include Beekman dolomite; Chazy, Black River, and Trenton limestones; and, Utica shale. Above these are the Silurian and Devonian formations, dating back to the days when the first fishes swam in the sea. Many marine fossils have been found in the sediment of the St. Lawrence lowlands, and in fact it is these remains that help scientists date the rocks which entomb them.

When the last layers of sediment were exposed and the sea was no more, erosion began to do its work, leveling and polishing the plain. But forces far below the surface were much more violent and abrupt. Between 100 and 125 million years ago, columns of hot, pressurized magma shot upwards through the sediment. This molten rock found its way into weak spots and fissures, creating what geologists call dikes and sills. Its main thrust was vertical, but the force behind these intrusions was not sufficient to send them bubbling through the surface. Thus, they cannot be called true volcanoes. Millions of years passed before their cooled, hard, igneous nubs appeared above ground, but the continuing erosion of the sedimentary plain finally assured them of their place in the local landscape. Another eon passed, and a creature with ideas named them the Monteregian Hills.

To the early Quebec settlers, the hills must have seemed like nuisances — something you had to plow around, and which could harbor a few lingering wolves and bears. By and large, they were left alone. Mt. St. Hilaire (Chapter 10) is a perfect

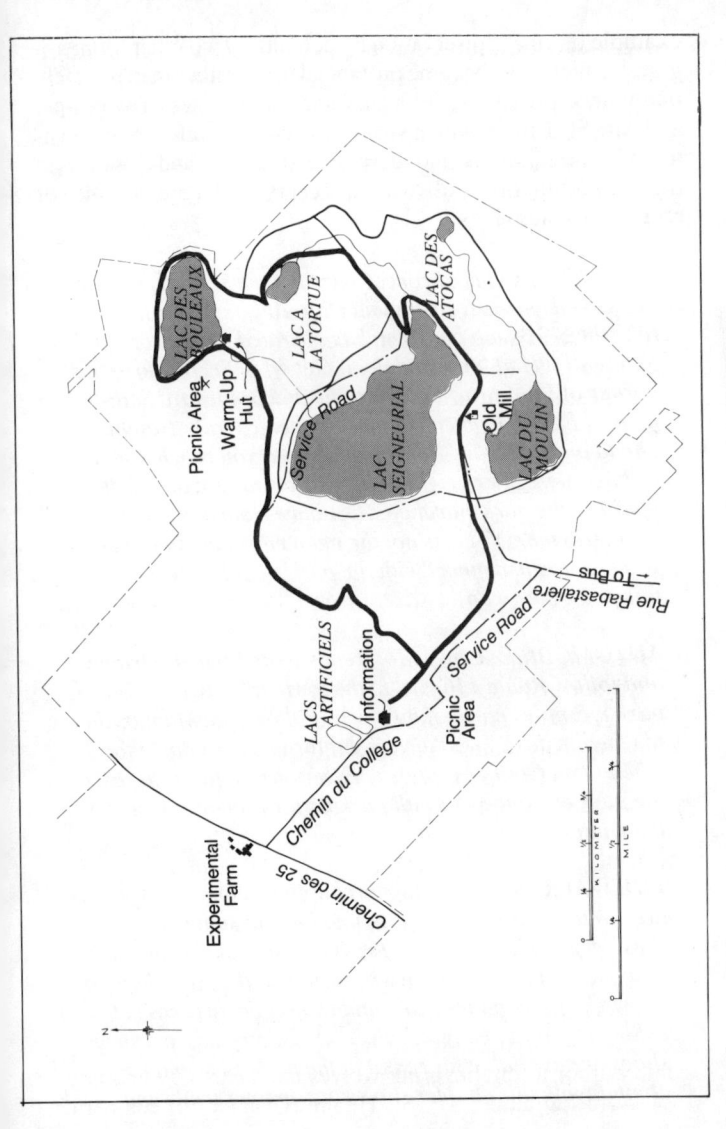

COUNTRY WALKS

example of this "preservation by default." Two other Monteregians, which have become provincial parks rather than privately maintained preserves, are Yamaska, in the Eastern Townships, and Mt. St. Bruno, which stands less than 15 miles from downtown Montreal. St. Bruno, despite its small size and closeness to the city, offers fine trails, varied scenery, and a broad choice of recreational activities.

PUBLIC TRANSIT: From Montreal, take Metro Line 4 to Longueuil, the last eastbound stop. At Longueuil station, take the St. Bruno bus, which is operated by Metropolitan Sud (call ahead for schedules). Get off in St. Bruno at the corner of Boulevard Boucherville and Boulevard Seigneuriel East. The bus will turn left here. Walk straight ahead on Boulevard Boucherville until you reach Rue Rabastaliere. Turn right on Rue Rabastaliere and walk uphill to the park entrance. (Distance from bus stop to park, 0.8 mile.) This is not the main entrance; however, you can easily connect with the park's trail system from this point (see map).

AUTOMOBILE: Leave Montreal via the Victoria Bridge and follow Route 116 east to the town of St. Bruno. The park is 2 miles north of the town. Follow Rue Montarville to Chemin des 25 and turn right; turn right again onto Chemin du College (opposite experimental farm) to reach the park entrance. A small parking fee is charged during the winter.

THE WALK: Not counting narrow connector routes, there are 3 main trails in Mt. St. Bruno Park in summer and 4 (Les Vergers, La Nordique, Les Bouleaux, and La Sucrerie) in winter. In addition, the winter map to the park shows a network of secondary trails and two separate areas set aside for snowshoeing. (Both cross-country skis and snowshoes are available for rental at the park.) The map accompanying this chapter shows the summer trails and

MOUNT ST. BRUNO

suggests a possible combination circuit. Other circuits are outlined in the map available at the park gate.

If you wish to take the route suggested here, follow Trail 1 for 1.2 miles, until you reach the shore of Lac Seigneuriel. At this point, you have the choice of going further on Trail 1 or taking the service road that curves along the lake.

The name of Mt. St. Bruno's largest lake is a reminder of the region's colonial past. Today, it seems to lend an air of feudal proprietorship to the elegant estates which dot the lake's southern margin. These homes and their grounds constitute the only private property on the south slopes of Mt. St. Bruno. If you walk along the lake, avoid trespassing by keeping to the service road or to the woods and meadows on your left.

Lac Seigneuriel is an important part of the watershed which serves the town of St. Bruno. Underground springs and feeder streams carry water to Lac des Bouleaux, farther up on the mountain. From there it flows to Lac Seigneuriel, and then to Lac du Moulin, after which the water is purified and enters the town's supply mains.

To reach the most isolated — and to many the most beautiful — part of Mt. St. Bruno Park, continue north of Lac Seigneuriel on Trail 1. A 0.6-mile walk will take you to higher ground, through a mixed hardwood forest in which the predominant species are beech, red oak, and the tree for which Lac des Bouleaux was named — the birch.

At Lac des Bouleaux you will find one of the three stove-heated warm-up huts which the park offers cross-country skiers. Here, also, is a picnic area, which makes a pleasant spot to stop and look at the birds. On a typical week in the spring of 1981, 80 species were sighted at Mt. St. Bruno. The park is either home or hunting ground to great blue herons, bald eagles, osprey, and kingfishers.

If you come in late spring or early summer and sit patiently near the banks of Lac des Bouleaux, you may get to see a little avian drama played out in one of the birch trees that lean out over the water. The old birches are riddled with the drillings of

COUNTRY WALKS

woodpeckers — the hairy woodpecker, in particular, is a common species here. The woodpecker will perforate a tree until its bark looks like a cribbage board, taking whatever insects it may find before flying off for another spot and beginning all over again. But that's not the end of the holes' usefulness. If sap is still flowing in the tree, ruby-throated hummingbirds may come by to take advantage of these ready-made "taps" which carry the sweet liquid to the surface. At Lac des Bouleaux, you can often see them hovering about the trunks of birches that have already served woodpeckers.

But, trouble starts when a hairy woodpecker decides that one of his old excavations might still harbor an insect or two, and discovers a hummingbird probing for sap. No matter how many holes there are, the two seem unable to coexist peacefully; the woodpecker invariably chases the hummingbird, and the hummingbird, with powers of flight that nearly defy physics, peels off to wait for another chance. When the woodpecker leaves, the hummingbird returns — and so on. As amusing as this territorial *pas de deux* may be, though, it serves to illustrate an important fact of forest management: a large individual tree can be many things to many species, and old growth past its prime should not be too relentlessly thinned if wildlife is to thrive.

Continue around Lac des Bouleaux, following the spur off Trail 3 that leads to Lac a la Tortue, the lake of the turtle. Snapping turtles abound in these small lakes, which makes it just as well that swimming is not permitted. Visitors are allowed to fish from shore, and the possible catch includes perch, bass, and catfish.

From where the Lac a la Tortue spur rejoins Trail 3, it is a walk of about ¾ mile back to the service road that encircles Lac Seigneuriel. Turn left at the lake shore, and follow the road past the private homes. Along the stream which flows between Lac Seigneuriel and Lac du Moulin stands the old structure which gives the latter body of water its name.

MOUNT ST. BRUNO

The mill at Lac du Moulin dates from the mid-eighteenth century, as does the triple-arch stone bridge which stands nearby. It was the first mill to be built in this area, and long served the *habitants* of the local seigneury. More recently, the building was used as a church. Although it stands empty today, park officials are discussing its adaptation as an information center, with public rest rooms. If funds are available, the wooden water wheel may even be replaced.

Near the mill and lake is a broad, well-kept lawn, ideal as a picnic spot. It was once a private three-hole golf course before being appropriated by the province and annexed to the park.

Finish the walk by continuing to the intersection of the road with Trail 3 (if you stay on the road, it will lead to the park gate at Rue Rabastaliere, which is the entrance most convenient to visitors arriving by bus). From here, it is another ¾ mile to the parking area and information building at the main park entrance. (Length of walk, excluding side trails, approximately 5½ miles.)

As you approach the end of your walk you will pass, on the left, a picnic grove which doubles as an apple orchard. Apples have been cultivated on Mt. St. Bruno's lower slopes since the early eighteenth century, and there are about 2,500 apple trees on the park grounds today. Most of them are picked by concessionaires and are off limits to visitors, but public picking is allowed on the 100 trees growing within the picnic area.

Mt. St. Bruno Park, Mt. Bruno de Montarville, Quebec, is open daily from 7 A.M. until sunset. For information, call 514-653-7544.

4

CAPE ST. JACQUES

Walking, ski touring, and snowshoeing — woods, meadows, and scenic coastline in a new 690-acre peninsular park maintained by the Urban Community of Montreal (CUM).

FEW PLACES ON THE ISLAND OF MONTREAL are more geographically obscure than Cape St. Jacques. A stubby thumb of land, it extends northward into the Lake of Two Mountains at the point where the Riviere des Prairies begins. It forces the river through the Cape St. Jacques Rapids, which separate the Cape from Ile Bizard by a scant 200 feet. It is about as far as you can get from Place Ville Marie without getting wet. It is a place guaranteed to provoke the question, "Where?"

Cape St. Jacques is so out-of-the-way that it is hard to find anyone with any idea of its history. There is a marker, near the intersection of Gouin Boulevard West and Anse a l'Orme, which tells of a seventeenth-century encounter with the Indians, but the Cape was so far away from the original settlements of Montreal that almost nothing else ever happened there. But now new history has been made by the Urban Community of Montreal's acquisition of Cape St. Jacques — from Gouin Boulevard to the water, on all sides — for use as a public park.

The CUM plan to preserve the Cape as open space has probably come not a moment too soon. In the nearby towns of Pierrefonds, Senneville, and St. Anne de Bellevue, signs of residential development are increasing and within a few years it will no doubt be impossible, if not prohibitively expensive, to

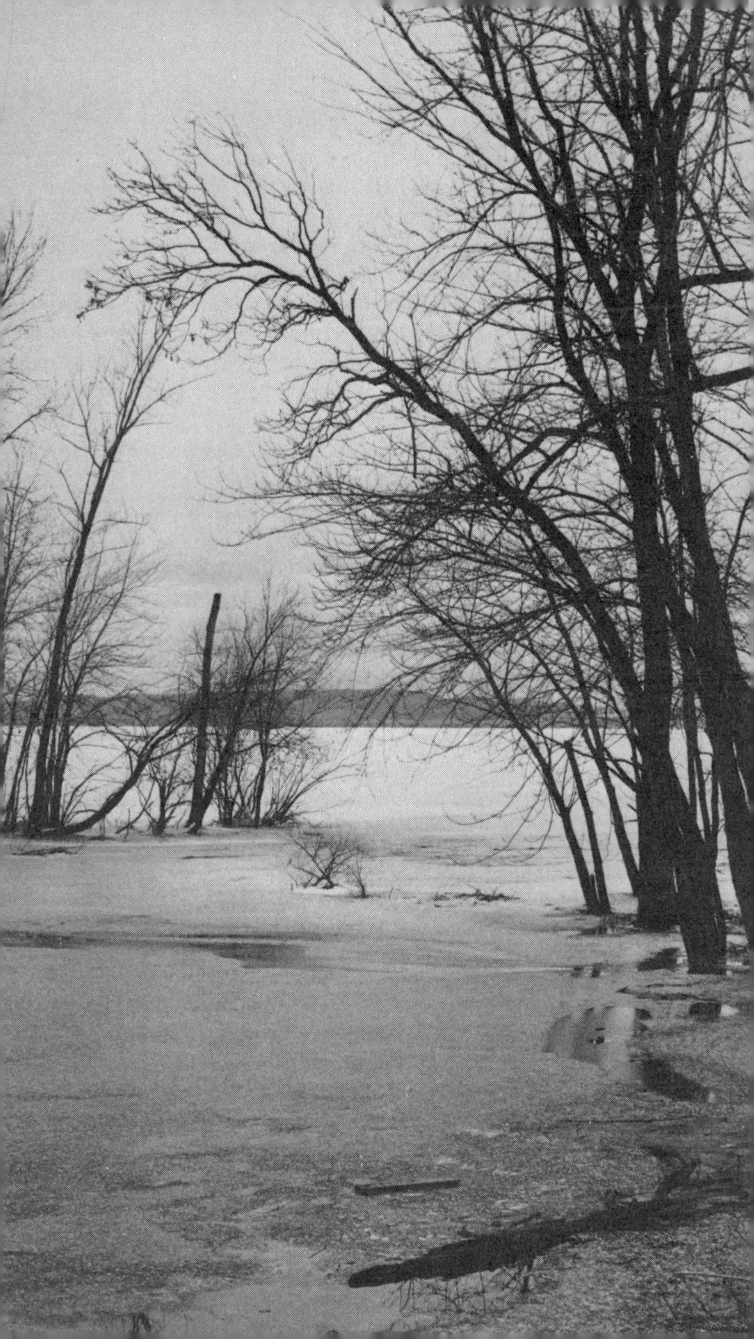

COUNTRY WALKS

acquire a tract as large and fine as Cape St. Jacques. There was a scattering of people living here, mostly near the northeast point; their houses and land were purchased by CUM and they were given ample time to move. Perhaps the largest property holder on the Cape was an order of nuns, the Sisters of the Holy Names of Jesus and Mary. The nuns were given a five-year tenancy following the park acquisition, and are due to leave by the end of 1983. No one is ever sanguine when it comes to eminent domain, but CUM had to make its move before suburban sprawl reached Cape St. Jacques. In the words of one CUM official, the woods and meadows of the new park "will give people a chance to see what this island was like 120 years ago."

PUBLIC TRANSIT: From the Henri Bourassa station, which is the last northbound stop on Metro Line 2, take the Number 69 bus westbound. Ask the driver for a transfer, and change for bus Number 68 at the end of the 69 line (ask driver for details). Take Number 68 west along Boulevard Gouin to the end of the line at Rue Chateau Pierrefonds. From here, continue on foot along Gouin Boulevard for approximately 1 mile, until you reach Chemin Cap St. Jacques. Turn right to enter the park. (Call ahead for bus schedules.)

AUTOMOBILE: From Montreal, take Route 40 (Metropolitan Boulevard) west until you reach the Boulevard St. Charles exit in Kirkland. Turn right onto Boulevard St. Charles, and follow it until it ends at Boulevard Gouin. Turn left onto Boulevard Gouin and continue to Chemin Cap St. Jacques, where you turn right to enter the park. An alternative is to drive the entire distance west on Boulevard Gouin, which is slower but offers a more varied look at the neighborhoods and open spaces which make up the western part of the island of Montreal.

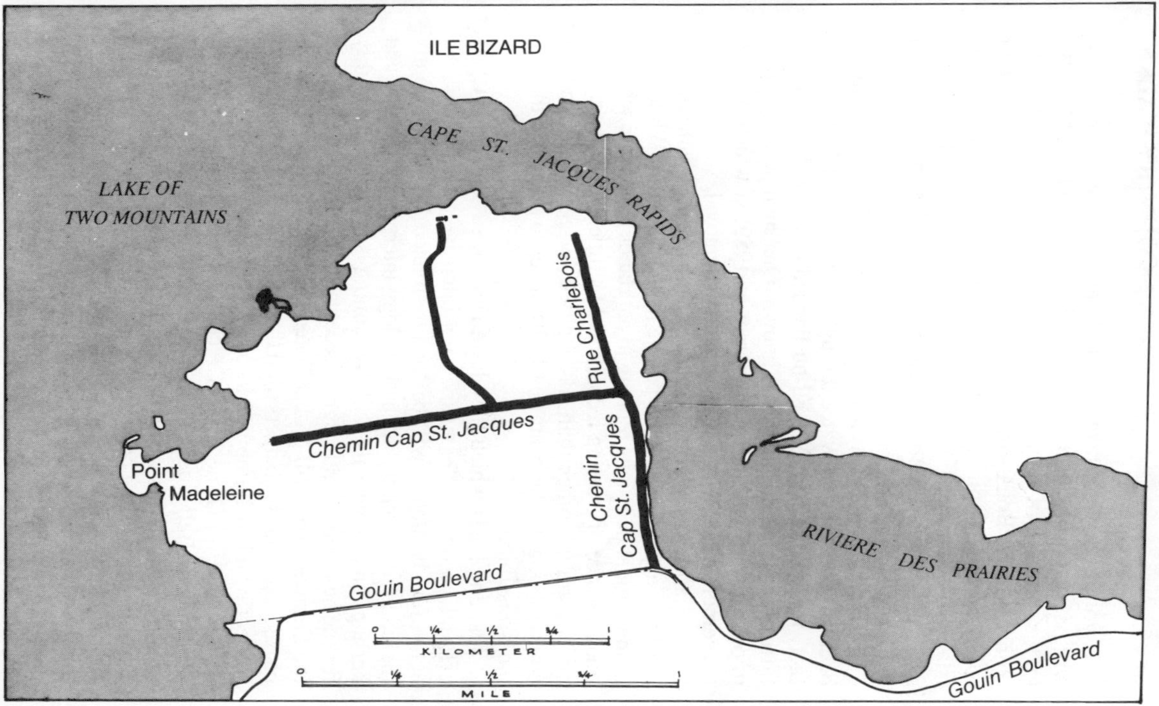
ILE BIZARD
CAPE ST. JACQUES RAPIDS
LAKE OF
TWO MOUNTAINS
Rue Charlebois
Chemin Cap St. Jacques
Chemin
Cap St. Jacques
Point
Madeleine
RIVIERE DES PRAIRIES
Gouin Boulevard
Gouin Boulevard
0 1/4 1/2 3/4 1
KILOMETER
0 1/4 1/2 3/4 1
MILE

COUNTRY WALKS

If you do drive or take the bus along Boulevard Gouin, you will pass a portion of the Saraguey Woods, which CUM is also in the process of acquiring for preservation. The Saraguey, which borders Boulevard Gouin for a ¾-mile stretch beginning at Boulevard Toupin, is part of the original climax forest of the island of Montreal. For whatever reason, it has survived nearly 350 years of settlement without being cut. It is truly an urban wilderness.

Cape St. Jacques has a somewhat tamer appearance, having been cut over and cultivated throughout the years. Much of it, in fact, retains the gentle, well-husbanded character of the horse farms for which this district is known. One such farm remained upon park ground until the summer of 1982, at which time an agreement made with CUM dictated its removal.

The park planning officials have been presented with what are hardly everyday options for people in their position. While most management decisions relating to parklands have to do with the maintenance of existing recreational facilities, CUM here faces no constraints other than those posed by geography and, of course, budget. Theirs are nearly 700 acres to make into the best park possible.

The emphasis which they have chosen, says a senior CUM official, is one of "extensive, not intensive, recreation." All activities, he notes, will be "nature-related." Plans currently include cross-country ski and ecology interpretation trails, and perhaps an orienteering trail. Swimming is a distinct possibility for the near future, although unacceptable water quality levels in the Ottawa River will probably keep Cape St. Jacques beaches closed to all but sunbathers until the mid-1980's. Another CUM project which will improve local water standards is the cleanup of the Anse a l'Orme (Elm) Creek, which flows north through St. Anne de Bellevue and empties into the Lake of Two Mountains near the park's western shoreline. Not only is CUM acquiring the shore of the cove stretching from Boyer Point to Point Madelene, but the agency's plans also include a greenbelt along the length of the Anse a l'Orme. It is hard to think about such a project without envisioning an eventual pedestrian and ski trail

CAPE ST. JACQUES

connecting Cape St. Jacques, Anse a l'Orme, and the Morgan Arboretum (Chapter 5).

For CUM, there is also the question of what to do with existing buildings on the Cape St. Jacques tract. Those which have architectural merit, or which are particularly sturdy, serviceable, and well-situated, will be converted to public use; many others will be razed. Planners have expressed special interest in the main building of the old convent complex, with one CUM spokesman favoring adaptation of the structure as a day-trip center for senior citizens — a concept, he notes, which has been ignored virtually everywhere else in North America.

THE WALK: With the exception of land belonging to a Catholic retreat house, all of Cape St. Jacques north of Gouin Boulevard is park property. During the early years of development, there might remain a few "No Trespassing" signs in parts of the park, but they can be safely ignored.

If you come to the Cape by bus, you will be in the park as soon as you turn from Gouin Boulevard onto Chemin Cap St. Jacques. After a ½-mile walk, with the rapids at your right and a meadow on your left, you will reach the parking area, where maps and information should be available. (Note: Have patience. As of this writing, the parking and information areas are planned for this area, but may not be in existence until 1983.)

If you drive to the park, you will already be at this location. From here you can walk directly down Rue Charlebois for ½ mile to the tip of the Cape, or you can follow Chemin Cap St. Jacques as it turns sharply to the left. This straight, tree-lined road suggests nothing so much as an allee *leading to a provincial manor in old France. It extends for just under a mile in the direction of Point Madelene, which juts crookedly into the Lake of Two Mountains.*

At a point about halfway along this final stretch of Chemin Cap St. Jacques, another road turns off to the

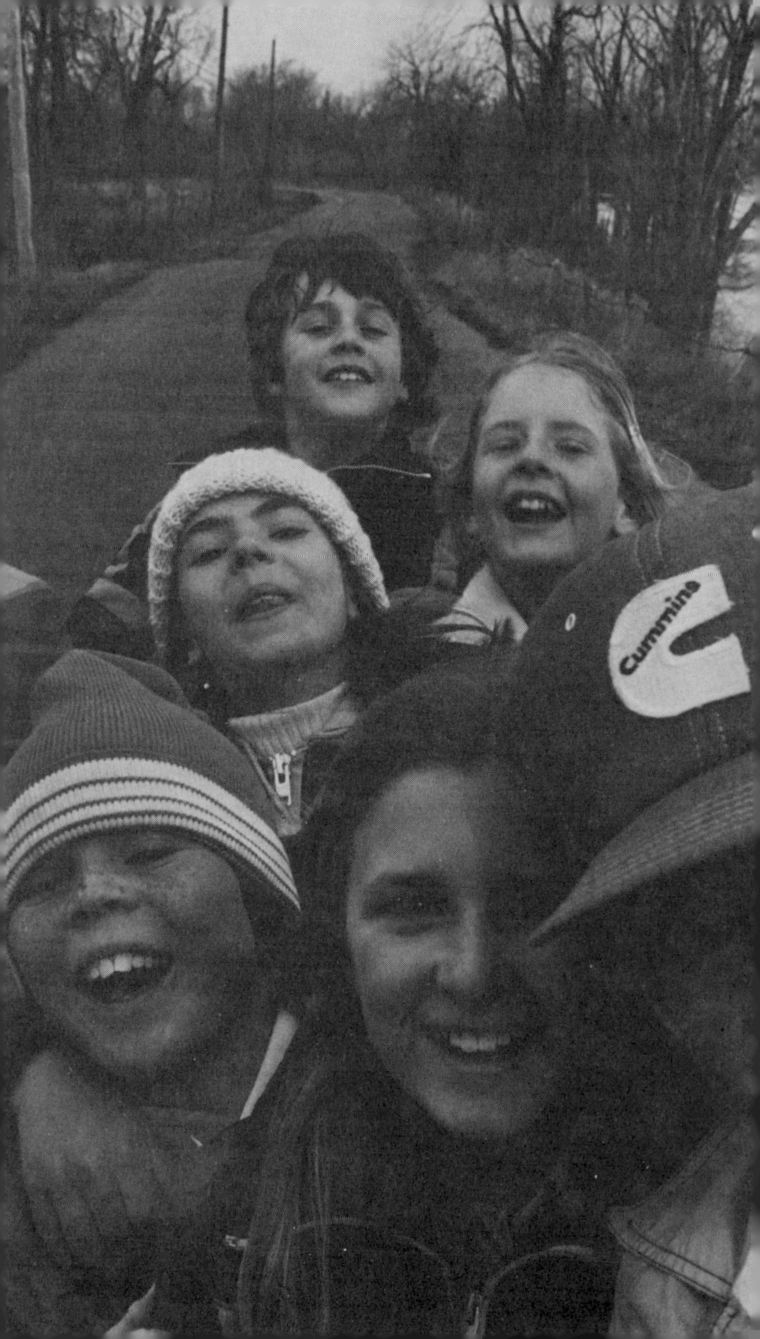
Cummins

CAPE ST. JACQUES

right. It curves through a pocket of forest and opens into old fields beginning to revert to second growth. At the opposite end of the field stand several of the old convent buildings, and beyond them, the Lake of Two Mountains.

It is fortunate that so many Montrealers said "Where?" for so many years when Cape St. Jacques was mentioned, and that CUM managed to acquire it before too many of them began to say "real estate." Now it can be preserved at that agreeable phase of development which lies halfway between forest primeval and urban park, and can serve as a reminder of the days when a short ride from Montreal was a ride into the country.

An outing at Cape St. Jacques

5

MORGAN ARBORETUM

Walking and ski touring — 12 miles of trails in a 600-acre arboretum near the western tip of Montreal Island. Tree species from throughout Canada grow here, in environments ranging from pocket wilderness to managed plantations.

LONG BEFORE THE FIRST EUROPEANS set foot in Canada, the ancestors of the Huron and Algonquin Indians were enjoying maple sugar. So important was this delicacy, which was believed to have been a gift from the Earth Mother Nokomis, that tribes living at some distance from large stands of maple trees would travel each year to maple country in anticipation of the running of the sap. So, it comes as a surprise to learn that the French settlers of Quebec learned nothing of the distillation of maple during the first hundred years after their arrival.

Strangely enough, it was a crisis in international commerce that brought about the general acceptance of what is now a staple of Quebecois cuisine. When war broke out between the British and the French in 1702, trade routes were severed, and the people of New France could no longer depend upon shipments of sugar from the West Indies. The situation was relieved by a Montreal gentlewoman named Madame Agathe de Repentigny. Having learned the secret of sugaring from the Indians, she offered it to the colonists as a substitute for the cane product. It was so readily and universally accepted that, within a few years, the island of Montreal alone was to account for an annual production of 30,000 pounds of maple sugar.

Boiling sap for maple syrup, Morgan Arboretum

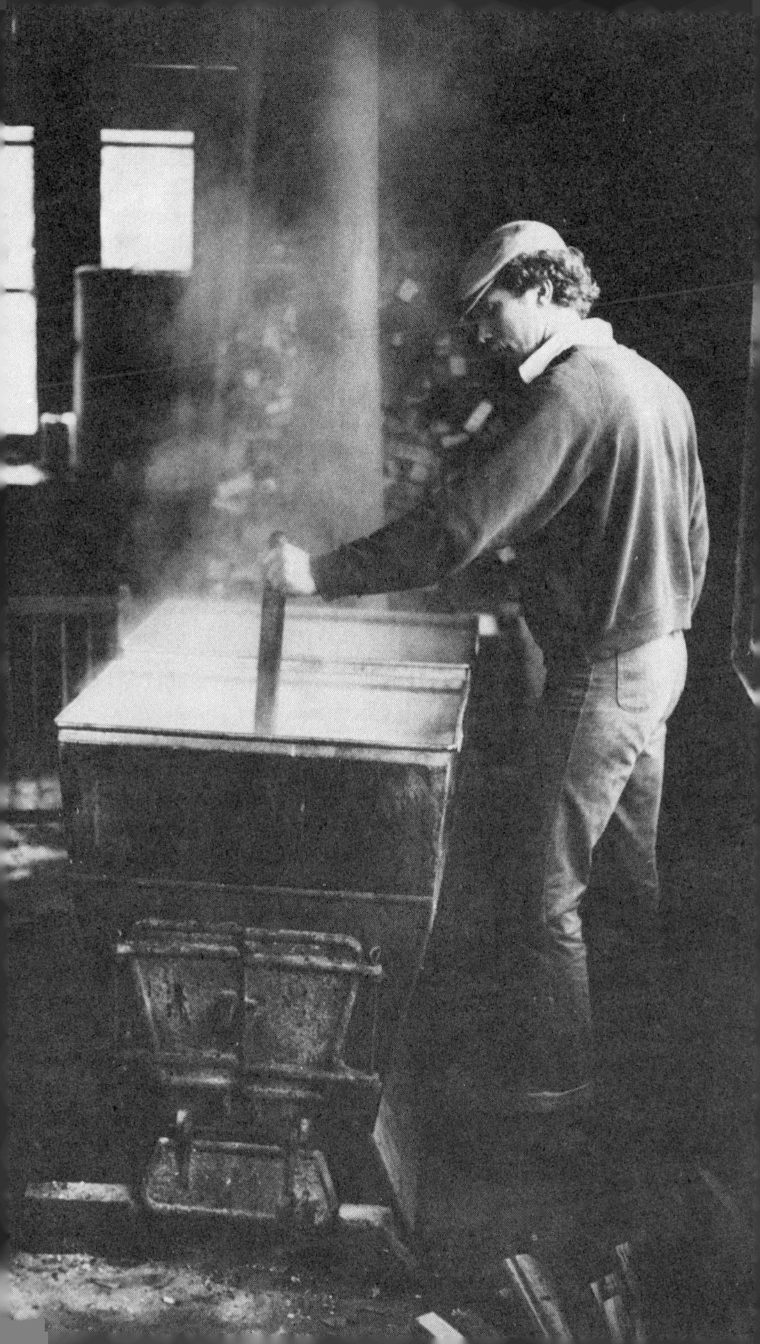

COUNTRY WALKS

At the Morgan Arboretum, in St. Anne de Bellevue, Macdonald College researchers have long since made up for the hundred-year lag that preceded Madame de Repentigny's "discovery." Here is where the use of pumps and plastic tubing for gathering sap was pioneered; here, late winter and early spring visitors can ski or hike to a working sugarhouse and observe man's age-old collaboration with Nokomis. It's all part of a program of management, education, and recreation that makes the Morgan Arboretum a model of Canada's forest resource.

Since it was founded in 1948, the arboretum has also come to represent the modern ideal of "multiple use" forest planning. Macdonald College, an agricultural school that is part of the McGill University system, assembled the tract out of an assortment of woodland acreage which had at one time or another been cultivated, cut for timber or firewood, or simply overlooked during the settlement of the still largely rural western portion of Montreal Island. The college's campus is less than three miles away, and the arboretum plays an important part in the education of future foresters and wildlife ecologists. Harvesting and sale of firewood, Christmas trees, maple products, and nursery stock serve to demonstrate the renewability of these resources and provide a source of income for the upkeep of the property. And, for walkers, skiers, and snowshoers, the college's discreet and unobtrusive stewardship of the arboretum makes it a fine place for a day's recreation.

PUBLIC TRANSIT: Although Voyageur (Ottawa lines) and Metropolitan Provincial (Numbers 21 and 21b) buses make the trip between Montreal's Voyageur station and St. Anne de Bellevue, their only St. Anne stop is at Rue St. Pierre and Route 20, which is reasonably convenient to the Macdonald campus but about 2½ miles from the arboretum. The same is true of C.P. Rail's Lakeshore service; the St. Anne station is just off Route 20, about 100 yards before the turnoff for Rue St. Pierre. (Saturday schedules are impossible and there are no trains on Sunday.) If you

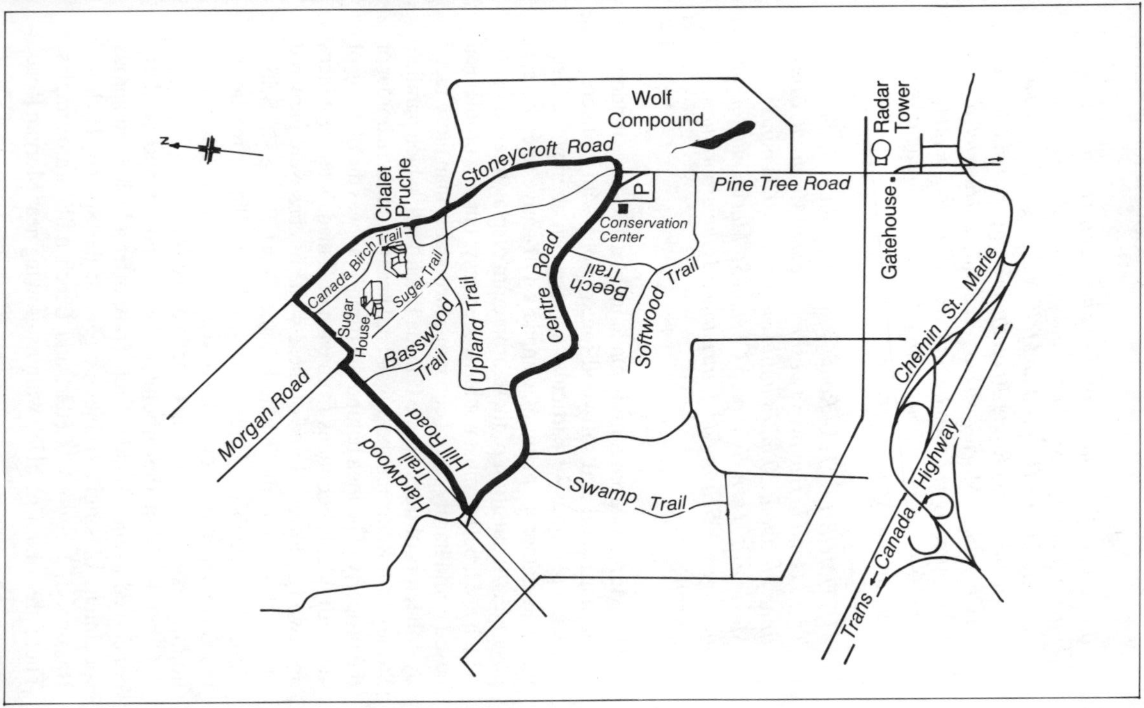
Wolf Compound
Stoneycroft Road
Pine Tree Road
Radar Tower
Gatehouse
P
Conservation Center
Chalet Pruche
Canada Birch Trail
Sugar Trail
Sugar House
Basswood Trail
Upland Trail
Centre Road
Beech Trail
Softwood Trail
Chemin St. Marie
Morgan Road
Hill Road
Hardwood Trail
Swamp Trail
Trans Canada Highway
N

COUNTRY WALKS

don't mind the walk — or if you have come by bicycle — turn right on Rue St. Pierre and go under the overpass; pass St. Anne's Hospital and follow the signs for Chemin St. Marie. Cross Route 40 on the overpass ramp, continue on Chemin St. Marie as it curves uphill, and turn left at the arboretum sign. Trails begin ½ mile from this point (2 miles from train and bus stops). If you have brought skis, you can put them on here.

AUTOMOBILE: Take Route 40 (Metropolitan Boulevard/ Trans Canada Highway) westbound out of Montreal. Continue for about 20 miles until you reach the Chemin St. Marie exit. Turn right onto Chemin St. Marie, and follow the signs indicating a left turn towards the arboretum entrance.

The Morgan Arboretum is made up of a 400-acre, randomly mixed hardwood and softwood forest, along with 200 acres of "block" plantings of particular species. An attempt has been made to gather as many of Canada's 170 native trees here as possible. Acquisition of these arboretum display trees, most of which are labeled, must not have been easy; but, the problems it posed could hardly have been more formidable than those faced by collectors of trees for the Canada Birch Trail, which parallels Stoneycroft Road and the Sugar Trail near the northern border of the property. The idea behind the Birch Trail was the planting of 400 individual specimens from each of Canada's ten provinces and two territories. Some of these white birches were garnered from places like the Klondike, the Coast Range of British Columbia, Quebec's Ungava peninsula, and the far reaches of the Gaspe. The project took six years to complete, and there is nothing like it elsewhere in Canada or the world.

Other trails in the arboretum, while not as spectacularly conceived as the Canada Birch Trail, offer a look at numerous specimens of single species or genera: the Spruce, Hickory, Basswood, Hemlock, Cedar, and Beech trails are examples. There are some fine black walnuts growing near Morgan Road,

MORGAN ARBORETUM

and the Birch Trail borders a planting of eastern white cedar, or arborvitae. Perhaps one of the arboretum's most unusual and unexpected sights, though, is a small stand of mature American chestnuts. These trees are growing in an isolated pocket north of their old range; that is why they have escaped the blight which devastated the species throughout the eastern United States. Look for them just off the Upper Hardwood Trail.

Other portions of the Morgan Arboretum bear the names, not of particular species, but of environments favorable to differing types of vegetation. There is an Upland Trail and a Swamp Trail, Hardwood Trails and a Softwood Trail. Near the intersection of the Beech Trail and the Centre Road, you will notice a mixed beech and maple climax forest. Both trees are highly shade tolerant, and intermingle to form the canopy in this part of the forest. Beeches differ from maples, however, in that they fare better on well-drained, sloping ground. On the flatter, south side of Centre Road, drainage is poorer, and you will notice the maples assuming greater predominance.

This section of Centre Road marks the southern boundary of the arboretum's 14-acre Ecological Reserve, a sector off limits to harvesting, debris removal, or other interference. It is, in effect, a wilderness, in which natural processes of growth, death, and decay take their course.

Conditions in the Ecological Reserve and in the remainder of the arboretum alike are favorable to wildflowers (350 species identified so far) and to birds. The great variety and numbers of birds here are a direct consequence of the abundance of fruit and nut-bearing trees. Small mammals, of course, also abound, but it is a larger one — the timber wolf — which has lately gotten most of the attention here.

Timber wolves? Haven't they been pushed back north of the Laurentians? Yes and no. The three wolves at the Morgan Arboretum were born in captivity, and they live in a three-acre compound just opposite the Conservation Centre and parking area. They are special charges of the Macdonald College Department of Renewable Resources Wildlife Group, for whom they do not always make things easy. As of this writing, there

COUNTRY WALKS

seems to be some disagreement between wolves and man on the matter of fences.

> *THE WALK: The Morgan Arboretum Conservation Centre and parking area are less than ½ mile beyond the gatehouse and radar weather station on Pine Tree Road. All trails lead from the parking area. During most of the year, the Conservation Centre is open; if it is not, pick up a map and ecology trail guide at the nearby self-service dispenser. Or, follow the map accompanying this text. A good cross-section of the arboretum may be observed by following Stoneycroft Road north from the parking area (all roads beyond this point are closed to vehicular traffic), past the Chalet Pruche, and towards the sugarhouse and Canada Birch Trail. Depending upon the weather, the sugarhouse can be active anytime from early March to early April. Turn left onto Morgan Road, then left again, after Morgan Road turns right, onto Hill Road. When you get to the dogleg in Hill Road (see map), turn sharply to the left to follow Centre Road back to the Conservation Centre. There are, of course, numerous side trails, some of which are better marked and maintained than others. In the winter, college officials usually select 3 trails of different lengths and blaze them with colored plastic ribbons. The trails change from year to year, so that impact is evenly distributed.*

If your drive to or from the arboretum takes you past the Macdonald campus, you may be interested in visiting two of the college's other attractions. One is the Lyman Entomological Museum in the MacDonald-Stewart Building. It houses over 1,000,000 insect and spider specimens, and is open daily by appointment (514-457-2000). The other is the Raptor Research Centre, dedicated to the study of birds of prey. Visits to the Raptor Centre are also by appointment only (514-457-9051).

Morgan Arboretum, MacDonald College, St. Anne de Bellevue, Quebec, is open during daylight hours throughout the

MORGAN ARBORETUM

year. During ski season, a weekend parking fee of $5.00 per car is charged; pedestrians pay $1.00. The summer fee is $3.00 per car. The above rates apply only to visitors who are not members of the Morgan Arboretum Association, a non-profit group established to help Macdonald College support this outdoor resource and its many conservation and educational programs. Parking and entry fees may be applied to membership dues on a one-time basis. Association members receive invitations to special events at the arboretum, and are entitled to discounts on maple syrup, Christmas trees, and other forest products. For information on membership, call 514-457-6580.

6

LONGUEUIL OUTDOOR CENTER/ CITY OF LONGUEUIL

Walking, ski touring, cycling, and a variety of other outdoor activities on a new 450-acre preserve, with 10 miles of trails, just across the St. Lawrence from Montreal. Later, a walk through the older precincts of Longueuil, where a number of historic buildings have been preserved.

THIS OUTING TAKES US TO THE OLD CITY of Longueuil on the south shore of the St. Lawrence, where the LeMoyne family once ruled over a wealthy and powerful seigneury. Charles LeMoyne, progenitor of the line, was one of the many adventurers who came from France during Montreal's early, "heroic" period to seek a name and fortune, and he was one of the few who succeeded. He arrived at Quebec in 1642, and like other able boys and young men — notably Pierre Boucher, of whom more is said in Chapter 13 — he was sent to live with the Hurons to learn their language and the lay of the Canadian land. LeMoyne mastered these lessons, which no doubt were put to good use during the campaigns which he led against the Iroquois. He must have been equally attentive to whatever arcane principles governed French colonial politics, because in 1657 Governor Lauzon awarded him the first of three land grants on the St. Lawrence shore opposite Montreal. Upon arriving to take possession of his new property, he gave it the name Longueuil, after a village in Normandy near Dieppe where he was born.

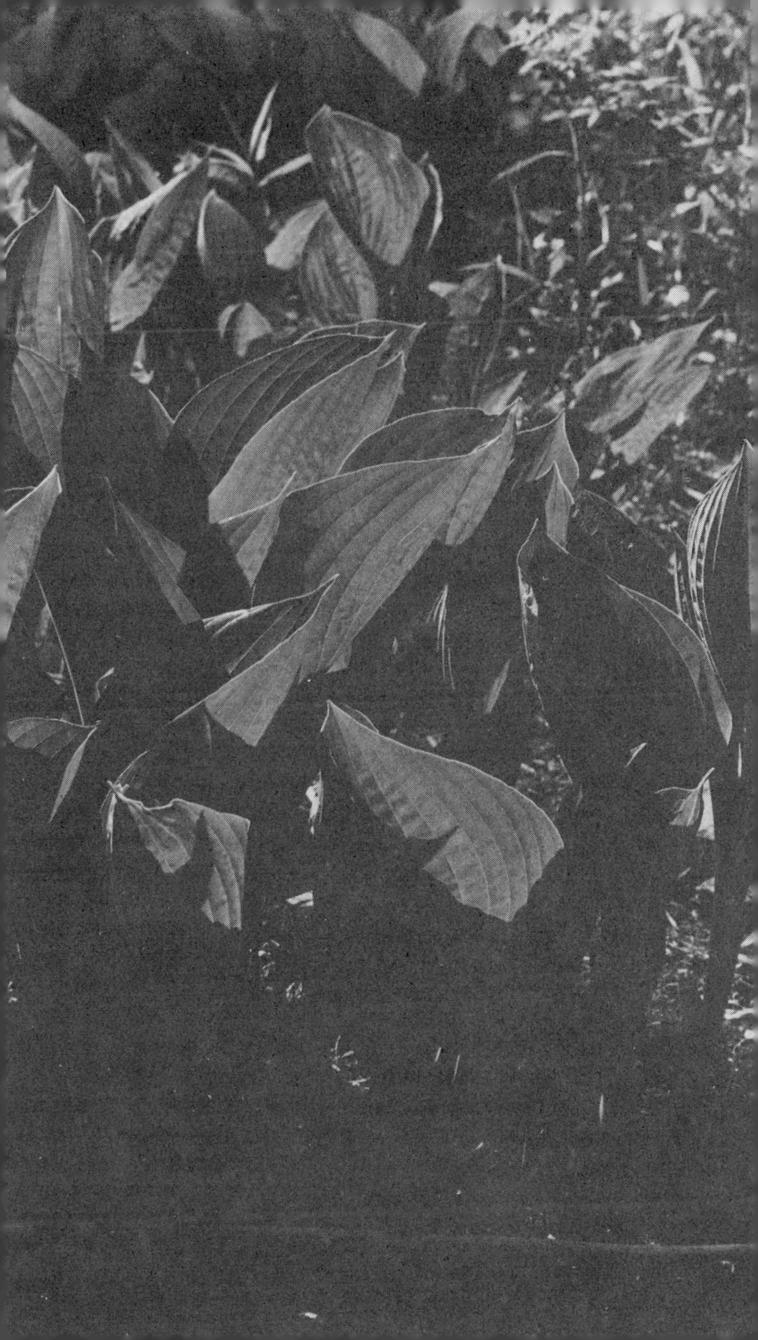

COUNTRY WALKS

In 1668, Longueuil officially became a seigneury, and in 1700 it was elevated to the status of a barony when Charles, eldest son of Charles LeMoyne, was granted a patent of nobility by Louis XIV. This first Baron de Longueuil assumed the local governorship in 1724. He succeeded Claude de Ramezay, for whom Old Montreal's Chateau de Ramezay, once the governor's residence and now a museum, was named. Several of the other LeMoyne sons, known by the various surnames which they took, were no less distinguished: d'Iberville explored the southern reaches of the Mississippi and gave the name Louisiana (for King Louis) to the land which he found there; and, de Bienville founded a settlement at the mouth of the great river. He named it New Orleans.

But, digression in both time and space is all too easy when talking about a family of such protean energy. In the late seventeenth century, much of this energy was still focused on the seigneury of Longueuil, where the old Indian fighter Charles LeMoyne had finally settled in 1666. In 1685, the year in which he died, work began on what was probably the mightiest private fortress in all of New France. The early seigneurs and the *habitants* who farmed their land were, in today's parlance, survivalists, but there was more of practicality than paranoia in their stance. Although by the 1680's the Iroquois were no longer a fate of everyday life in and around Montreal, they were still capable of lightning guerrilla-style raids, as witness the horrible Lachine massacre of 1689 and the attacks on Pointe aux Trembles in the early 1690's. The LeMoynes wanted security at Longueuil, and they achieved it in the form of a huge stone complex which owed more to the feudal style of the Old World than to the emerging farmhouse architecture of Quebec. The square, two-story structure, with four squat, round towers at its corners, surrounded and protected an elaborate manor house, along with a church, mill, stables, and outbuildings. It was called the Chateau de Longueuil, and it stood for over 100 years. Ironically, this bastion built by the French as a defense against the Indians later became a prize in the struggle between two other antagonists, the British and the Americans. American

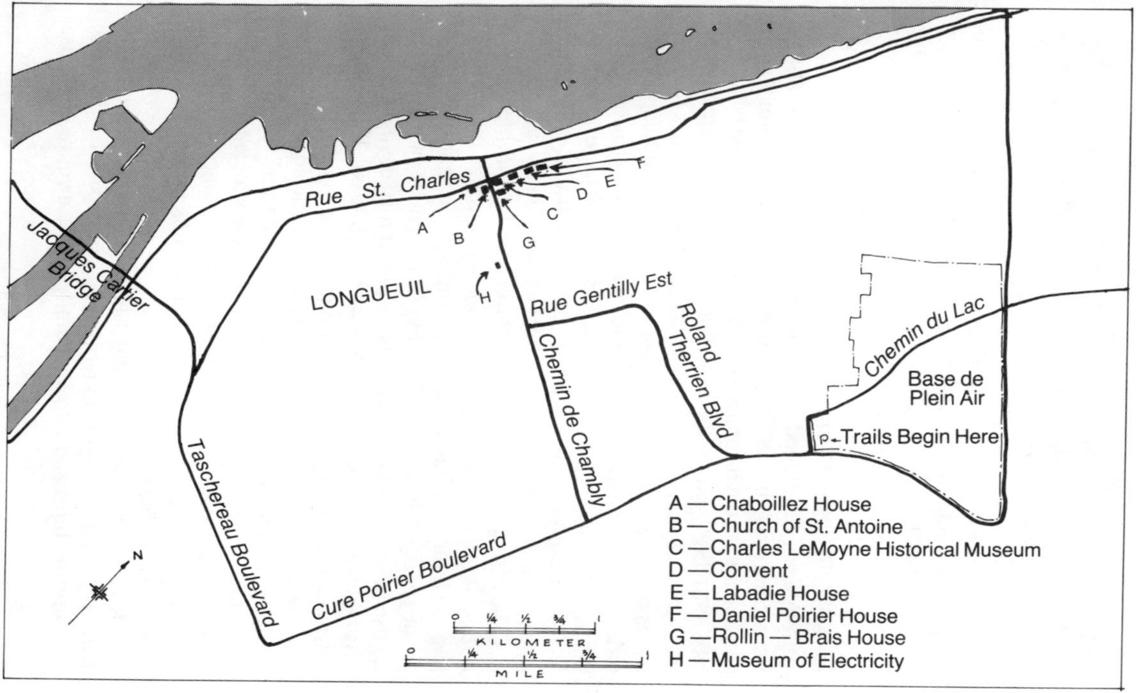
Rue St. Charles
Jacques Cartier Bridge
LONGUEUIL
Rue Gentilly Est
Roland Therrien Blvd
Chemin de Chambly
Chemin du Lac
Base de Plein Air
P Trails Begin Here
Taschereau Boulevard
Cure Poirier Boulevard
N
0 1/4 1/2 3/4 1
KILOMETER
0 1/4 1/2 3/4 1
MILE
A — Chaboillez House
B — Church of St. Antoine
C — Charles LeMoyne Historical Museum
D — Convent
E — Labadie House
F — Daniel Poirier House
G — Rollin — Brais House
H — Museum of Electricity

COUNTRY WALKS

invaders occupied Longueuil early in the Revolution; in fact, it was from here that Ethan Allen launched his abortive assault on Montreal. Later, with the forces of "liberation" routed from Canada, the British occupied the old stone fortress. Soon, it would belong to no one — in 1792, fire reduced the complex to broken walls and rubble. The ruins were demolished and largely removed during the early 1800's, and in 1814 the remaining stones were used to build a church on the chateau site. That site is now occupied by the 1885 Church of St. Anthony, in whose masonry fragments of the chateau still exist.

Longueuil developed slowly during the nineteenth century. As recently as the 1880's, it was still regarded mainly as a convenient yet quiet summer resort. Longueuil did not become a city until 1920, but in the years since it has been no stranger to industry and expansion. Like Montreal, Longueuil has found it necessary to launch a movement to restore the buildings in its oldest downtown quarter. But, the city's attention has turned to the need for saving what open spaces remain on its periphery, as well as preserving the heirlooms at its core. It was in appreciation of that need that the Longueuil Outdoor Center was created.

(The official, French name of the center, *Base de plein air de Longueuil*, incorporates an idiom, *plein air,* which might translate most directly into English as "full air" or "complete air." Some sense of the connotations of *plein* might be gathered from its use in other idioms, such as *plein jour* (broad daylight); *plein hiver* (dead of winter); and, *plein mer* (high seas). The sense is always carried of a presence or commodity at its fullest, or most intense; thus *plein air* refers to a fullness, a repleteness of air that is not apparent in confined places. "Open air" might be a reasonable English equivalent, although the simple term "outdoors" corresponds most directly with the concept of places such as this one, at Longueuil, and the Les Forestiers Center described in Chapter 16.)

The Longueuil Outdoor Center is an ambitious project, only partially complete, which involves the conversion of 450 acres of one-time farmland into a naturally landscaped, multiple-use

LONGUEUIL

recreation facility. The city owns the property, and it is the city which has undertaken its development. Final plans call for the creation of two lakes, both near the Cure Poirier Boulevard/Rue Adoncour entrance, one of which will be open to swimmers and skaters. As of this writing (summer, 1981), one of the lakes has already been excavated. The earth which was removed has been used to build a toboggan slide and a small downhill ski slope. Remember, these are the St. Lawrence lowlands, where the vertical dimension would be virtually nonexistent were it not for the Monteregian Hills and minor alterations such as these.

The predominant activities at the center, though, are walking, cycling, snowshoeing, and ski touring. It has been the practice during recent winters to color-blaze and pack three interconnected ski trails, totaling approximately 10 miles. Snowshoers have the run of some 400 wooded acres — virtually the entire area — but should stay clear of those trails which are maintained for skiing. Bring all necessary equipment, since rentals are not part of the city's plans for the center.

In summer, all of the same trails are open to walkers, and some will be marked for cyclists. By 1983, the center's developers hope to offer guided nature walks. Whether you go with a guide or not, take your bird book — over 100 species have been sighted here.

PUBLIC TRANSIT: From Montreal, take Metro Line 4 to Longueuil Station. From the station, take the Number 8 bus to the intersection of Cure Poirier Boulevard and Chemin de Chambly. Transfer to the Number 7 bus and get off at Cure Poirier Boulevard Est and Rue Adoncour, where the center entrance is located.

AUTOMOBILE: Leave Montreal via the Jacques Cartier Bridge. When you reach Longueuil, bear right onto Taschereau Boulevard. Follow Taschereau for approximately 1¼ miles, and exit left onto Cure Poirier Boulevard Ouest. Follow Cure Poirier Boulevard for approximately

COUNTRY WALKS

2½ miles; shortly after you cross a major intersection, you will reach Rue Adoncour and the entrance to the center. Parking space is available here.

THE WALK: Trails begin near the Cure Poirier Boulevard/Rue Adoncour entrance to the center. You can also walk or cycle along the Chemin du Lac, which begins at Rue Adoncour 1 block up from Cure Poirier Boulevard, and which bisects the center property. Since development of the center is still underway, and since trail designations may change, it is not possible to give specific directions here. In winter, follow the color-coded trail blazes; in summer, should trails not be marked, just remember that the entire center is surrounded by paved roads, and that you are not likely to get lost. To request the most recent maps of the center, call or write the Longueuil Direction du loisir (department of recreation) at the address given at the end of this chapter.

Having spent time enjoying Longueuil's natural attractions, you may have time left for a look at some of the city's architectural and historical points of interest. "Old Longueuil," the compact quarter which lies near the river, is approximately two miles distant from the Outdoor Center.

PUBLIC TRANSIT: From the center entrance, return to the intersection of Cure Poirier Boulevard and Chemin de Chambly via the Number 7 bus. Old Longueuil is to your right, approximately 1½ miles down Chemin de Chambly. The Number 8 or Number 88 bus will take you there.

AUTOMOBILE OR WALKING: From the Outdoor Center entrance, follow Cure Poirier Boulevard to Rolland Therrien Boulevard, turn right, and walk or drive approximately ¾ mile to Rue Gentilly Est. Turn left and continue on Gentilly for less than ¼ mile; then turn right onto

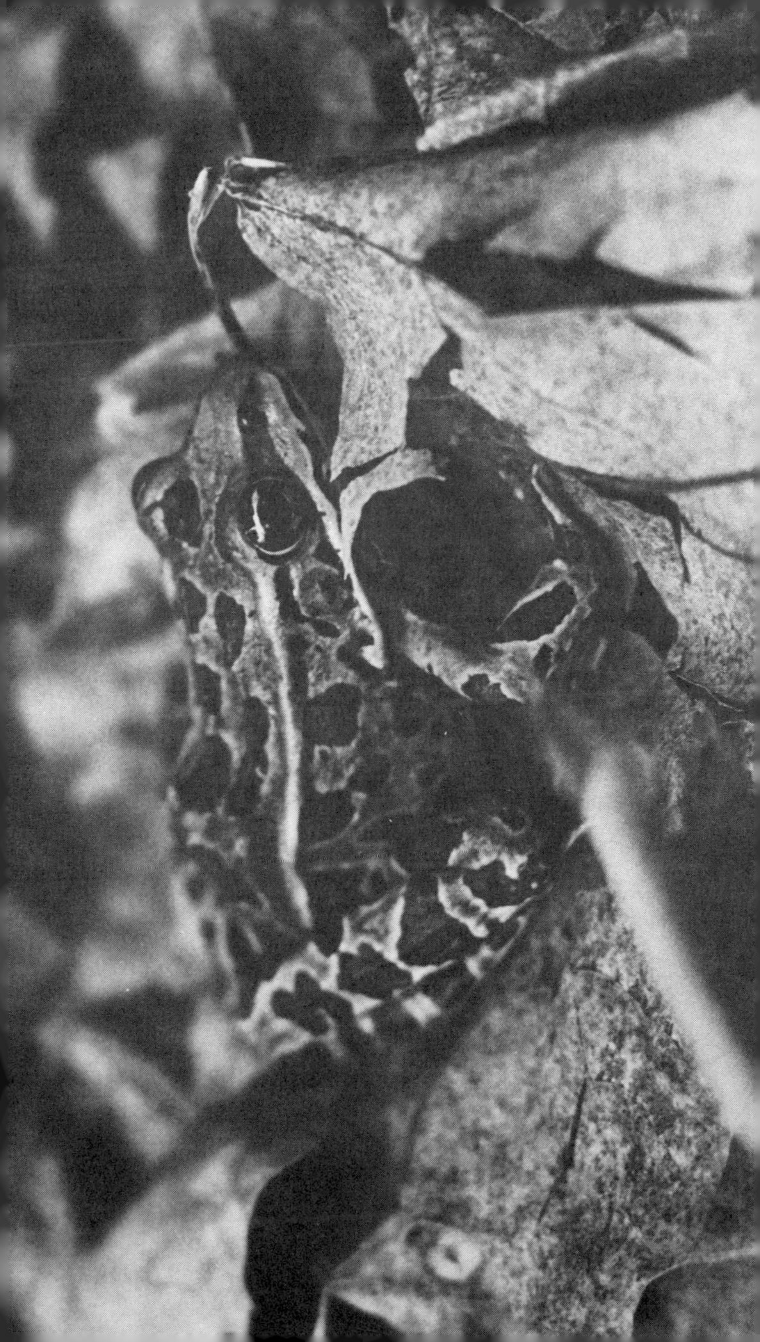

COUNTRY WALKS

Chemin de Chambly, which leads directly into Old Longueuil.

What to see in Old Longueuil? There are two small museums, a church, and several interesting houses within a few blocks of the intersection of Chemin de Chambly and Rue St. Charles. At 4 St. Charles Est, in the Bank d'epargne, is the Charles LeMoyne Historical Museum. The museum, which is open during banking hours (including Thursday evenings until 8), houses a collection of old silver, home furnishings, books, coins, and articles relating to the early history of Longueuil. Almost directly opposite the museum, facing St. Charles, is the Church of St. Antoine. This is the church which stands on the site of the Chateau de Longueuil, and which incorporates some of the chateau's stones in its walls. The interior of the church is ornate and colorful, with paintings by the Quebecois artist Jean-Baptiste Roy-Audy. In the crypt of St. Antoine are the tombs of several locally prominent families, including the LeMoynes.

Next to the church, on St. Charles near Grant Avenue, stands the Chaboillez House. This stately and harmonious stone building, with its neoclassical portico, was built as a rectory in 1815. It first belonged to Father Chaboillez, pastor of St. Antoine, and long served various church functions. Today, it houses an art gallery and the studios of local craftsmen.

Walk back across Chemin de Chambly and continue along St. Charles. You will pass, on your right, the Convent of the Sisters of the Holy Name of Jesus and Mary, part of which dates to 1769; the Labadie House, built in 1834 of stone from the old chateau; and, the tidy little Daniel Poirier House, known to have been built before 1750 and believed to be the oldest dwelling in Longueuil.

Now retrace your steps along St. Charles, returning again to its intersection with Chemin de Chambly. Turn left on Chambly. At the end of the block (corner of Rue St. Andre), on your left stands the 1798 Rollin-Brais House, which once served as a forge and later as an inn. It has recently been restored by the

LONGUEUIL

city. Continue for several blocks to reach Number 440 Chemin de Chambly, where you will find the small but fascinating Museum of Electricity. The museum (open Tuesday to Friday from 10 A.M. to 5 P.M., weekends 11 to 5) houses a collection amassed over 50 years by a Longueuil electrician, Gaston LaBadie. It includes early household appliances and office equipment of every description, from the first vacuum cleaners and toasters to a 1905 Edison dictating machine.

If you are driving, return along St. Charles Ouest to the Cartier Bridge approaches. To reach the Metro station by bus, take the Number 8 or Number 88, both of which run along Chemin de Chambly, turning left at St. Charles.

The Longueuil Outdoor Center (*Base de plein air*) is administered by the Longueuil Direction du loisir, 360, Rue Cherbourg, Longueuil, Quebec. Call 514-679-6490 for information.

7

PARC ANGRIGNON-LACHINE CANAL

Ski touring, bicycling, and walking — 4¾ miles, each direction. Beginning at Angrignon Park, the ski touring route continues along an historic canal to the city of Lachine, once the eastern terminus of the fur trade.

A CROSS-COUNTRY SKI TRIP need not involve a long drive out of town, nor does it have to consist of going around in circles on the grounds of a small city park. This route begins in a park (a fairly large one, actually), but veers off to parallel the old Lachine Canal, which bisects that part of Montreal Island that bulges southward towards the Lachine Rapids. After a couple of miles, it ends in Lachine, where the St. Lawrence River widens to become Lake St. Louis.

When there is no snow on the ground, the paved pathway along the canal makes just as good a route for walkers and cyclists. However, the directions given below do not exactly apply when the canal is not frozen. Because there is no year-round bridge access from the waterway's south bank, a different approach to the pathway is necessary during the warmer seasons. There are several, as any city map will suggest — just remember that the Canadian National Railway yards block access to the canal along a good part of its north bank.

PUBLIC TRANSIT: To reach Angrignon Park from downtown Montreal, take Metro Line 1 to Angrignon station, which is the last stop for westbound trains. Make your way

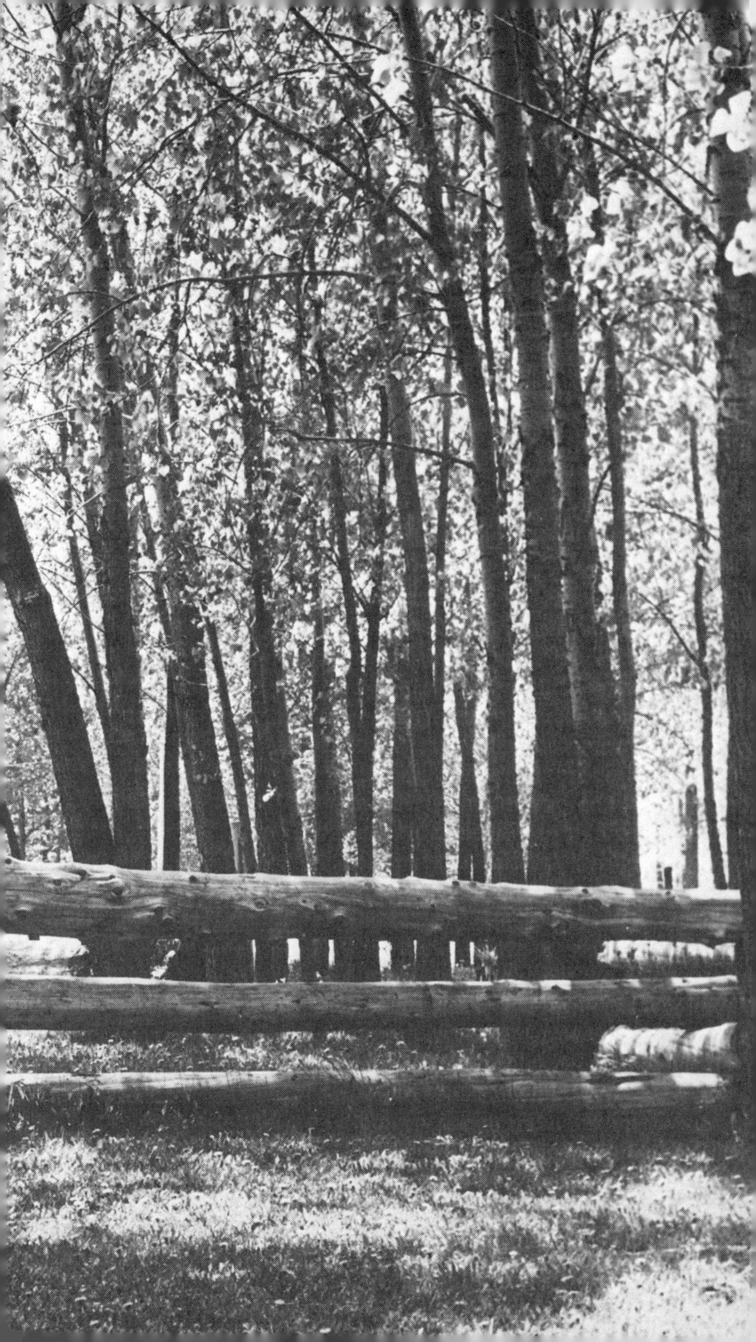

COUNTRY WALKS

directly across the park, past the skating area to the tip of the long, narrow lake that stretches diagonally across the park. Near here you will be able to pick up the red- and yellow-blazed trail that leads towards the canal (see below).

If you ski (or walk) all the way to Lachine and do not wish to backtrack, pick up the Number 191 bus on Notre Dame Street, downtown Lachine, and ride back to the Place St. Henri station on Metro Line 2. You can also catch the 191 at the intersection of Notre Dame and Gauron Boulevard, a short distance north of the point where the paved path switches to the south bank of the canal (see map).

AUTOMOBILE: To reach the parking lot which marks the beginning of the route described below, approach Angrignon Park from de la Verendrye Boulevard, which runs along the park's southern border. There are several ways of getting to de la Verendrye from downtown Montreal, all of which involve crossing the Lachine Canal and none of which are easily described. Here, again, a city map is suggested.

THE SKI TOUR: From the rear of the de la Verendrye Boulevard parking lot in Angrignon Park, turn left onto the trail blazed with red and yellow markers. The skating rink will be on your right, as will be the dome of St. Joseph's Oratory some 3 miles distant. Bear right around the tip of the lake. You will soon see a small pavilion on your left. At this point, you have the option of continuing the circuit of Angrignon Park, or striking off for the canal. To reach the canal, turn left and ski past the rear of the pavilion, continuing to a gate in a cyclone fence that stands just before the Canadian Pacific Railroad tracks. Carefully cross the tracks, and proceed straight ahead across a field towards Newman Boulevard. As you cross the field, keep the woods close by on your right.

Remove your skis and cross Newman Boulevard. Then

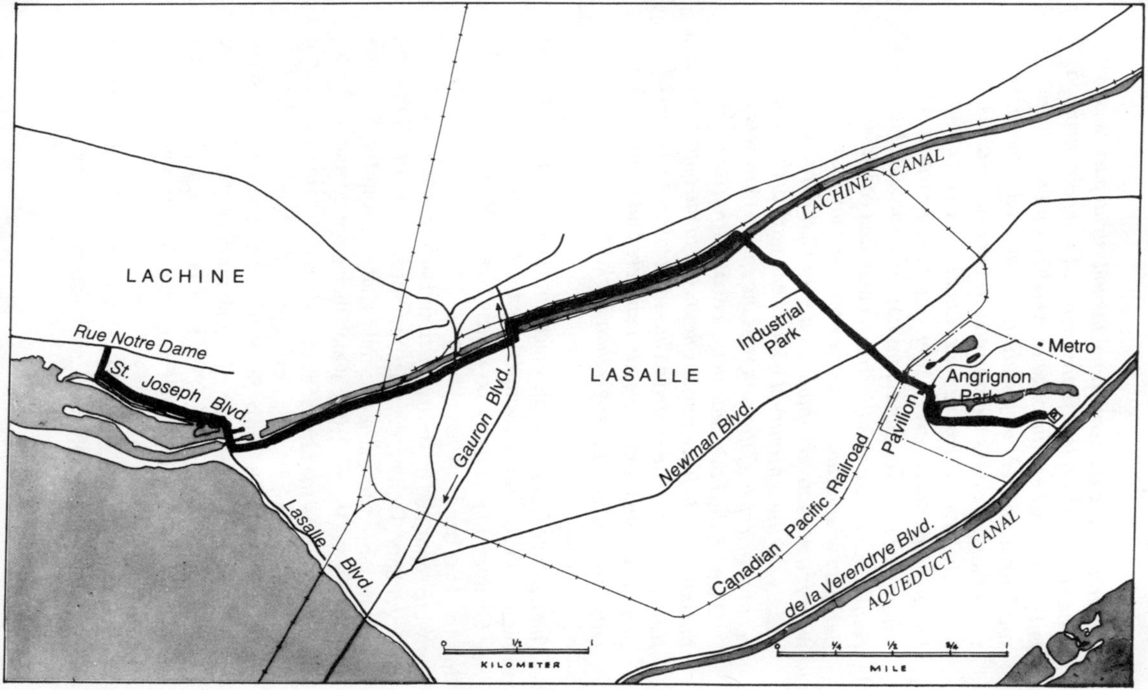
LACHINE
LASALLE
Rue Notre Dame
St. Joseph Blvd.
Lasalle Blvd.
Gauron Blvd.
Newman Blvd.
Industrial Park
LACHINE CANAL
Canadian Pacific Railroad
Pavilion
Angrignon Park
Metro
de la Verendrye Blvd.
AQUEDUCT CANAL
0 1/2 1
KILOMETER
0 1/4 1/2 3/4 1
MILE

COUNTRY WALKS

continue straight ahead along the industrial park access road (factories on left, fields on right) to a point about ½ mile farther where the road turns left. Don't follow the road; head straight across the field until you come to the slope that overlooks the railroad tracks and canal. You'll probably have to remove your skis to descend the slope — but the hard part is over. After you cross the tracks, you will notice that wooden ramps have been provided to enable skiers to cross the frozen canal and reach the pathway which runs along the opposite shore. Don't worry; the relatively shallow Lachine Canal freezes quite solidly during a Montreal winter, and park authorities remove or rope off the ramps as the spring thaw sets in.

Once on the other side of the canal, turn left and follow the path. If you have any suspicions as to the improvisational nature of the route you have just taken, rest assured: there is a sign along the path near here that points to the canal and says, "To Angrignon Park."

The Lachine Canal was the nineteenth century's answer to the problem solved, in the twentieth by the St. Lawrence Seaway (See Chapter 11). But, by no means was it the first attempt to link the two heads of navigation — Montreal and Lachine — that were separated by the treacherous Lachine Rapids. In 1689, the legendary Dollier de Casson, Superior of the Sulpician Order, proposed to cut a one-mile channel from the St. Lawrence to the St. Pierre River, which then emptied into the larger stream just below the rapids. His idea was to provide a navigable route for canoes, as well as to increase the flow of water that powered mills on the little St. Pierre. The Lachine Massacre (see below) made execution of the plan impossible, but twelve years later he tried again. This time he hired a professional engineer and got the work half finished before his own religious superior ordered him to stop.

A century passed, and still the Lachine Rapids stood in the way of navigation on the St. Lawrence. But, as the nineteenth

PARC ANGRIGNON-LACHINE CANAL

century dawned, competition between Canada and the newly independent United States forced both sides into planning ways of improving the efficiency of their east-west trade routes. Military transport was also a factor, as the War of 1812 showed.

America's answer was the Erie Canal, begun in 1817. New York, in particular, had been jealous of the increasing dependence of American northwestern settlements on Canadian routes, such as that afforded by the St. Lawrence. With the new Albany-to-Buffalo route, it could offer stiff competition to Canadians, who were still obliged to portage goods overland around the Lachine Rapids. It was time to revive the idea of a Lachine Canal.

A private company was chartered in 1819 to get the job started, but its finances were shaky and the Canadian government had to take over. By then — the year was 1821 — businessmen and civic leaders along the St. Lawrence valley knew that an entire system of canals was needed between Montreal and the Great Lakes. The Lachine project was to be the rallying point for this tremendous effort.

Work on the canal got under way in the summer of 1821. The new government commission scrapped the original plan for a 12-mile waterway that would extend all the way to the foot of the St. Mary current, downstream from the port, in favor of the present 8½-mile route. The canal was to be five feet deep, with six locks to ease boats down its 45-foot drop. There would be a towpath along the north bank, so that draft animals could haul barge traffic.

It took nearly six years to build this first Lachine Canal. As it turned out, the same igneous rock that formed the rapids lay below the surface in the excavators' path, and three miles of the route had to be dearly purchased with dynamite. Flooding was also a recurrent dilemma. But, the finished product was a handsome, cleverly engineered, and sturdily built canal, with locks made entirely of stone — the only such installations in all of North America. Montrealers were proud of this fine new public work. They walked along its banks on Sunday after-

COUNTRY WALKS

noons, and enjoyed two-hour canal cruises aboard the *Jane*, a passenger boat built especially for the canal.

The first Lachine Canal was quickly outmoded, both because of the increasing traffic it generated and the new steamboats, which it could not accommodate. Between 1843 and 1848, a new canal was built alongside the old; this is the one along which we can walk, ski, and cycle today. But, obsolescence catches up with all the works of man, particularly if they have to do with commerce. Modern shipping is carried through the St. Lawrence Seaway; in fact, highway building has even caused the eastern approach of the Lachine Canal to be blocked with fill. There has been talk of reviving the old waterway as a through route for pleasure craft, but it is likely to be quite a while before any such improvements are made.

> *A little over a mile from where you first crossed the canal, you will see two red cabooses permanently sided on a track to the left of the path. On the side of one caboose is a map of the canal and the entire trail system. Here, also, is where you must unbind your skis and walk across the Gauron Boulevard bridge to where the path continues on the opposite bank.*
>
> *Another mile and a half brings you to another bridge, which marks the end of the Lachine Canal and its accompanying path. Rather than turn right around, though, it is worthwhile to continue on foot into the town of Lachine, one of the oldest and most famous of all St. Lawrence River settlements. To reach the town center, cross the Lasalle Boulevard bridge and turn left onto St. Joseph Boulevard. On your left is a skating rink and waterfront park; soon, you will come upon an ancient stone building which was once a warehouse of the Hudson's Bay Company.*

In the early 1800's, Lachine was the headquarters of the Hudson's Bay Company, and before that it was the home port of the North West Company, which the surviving firm challenged

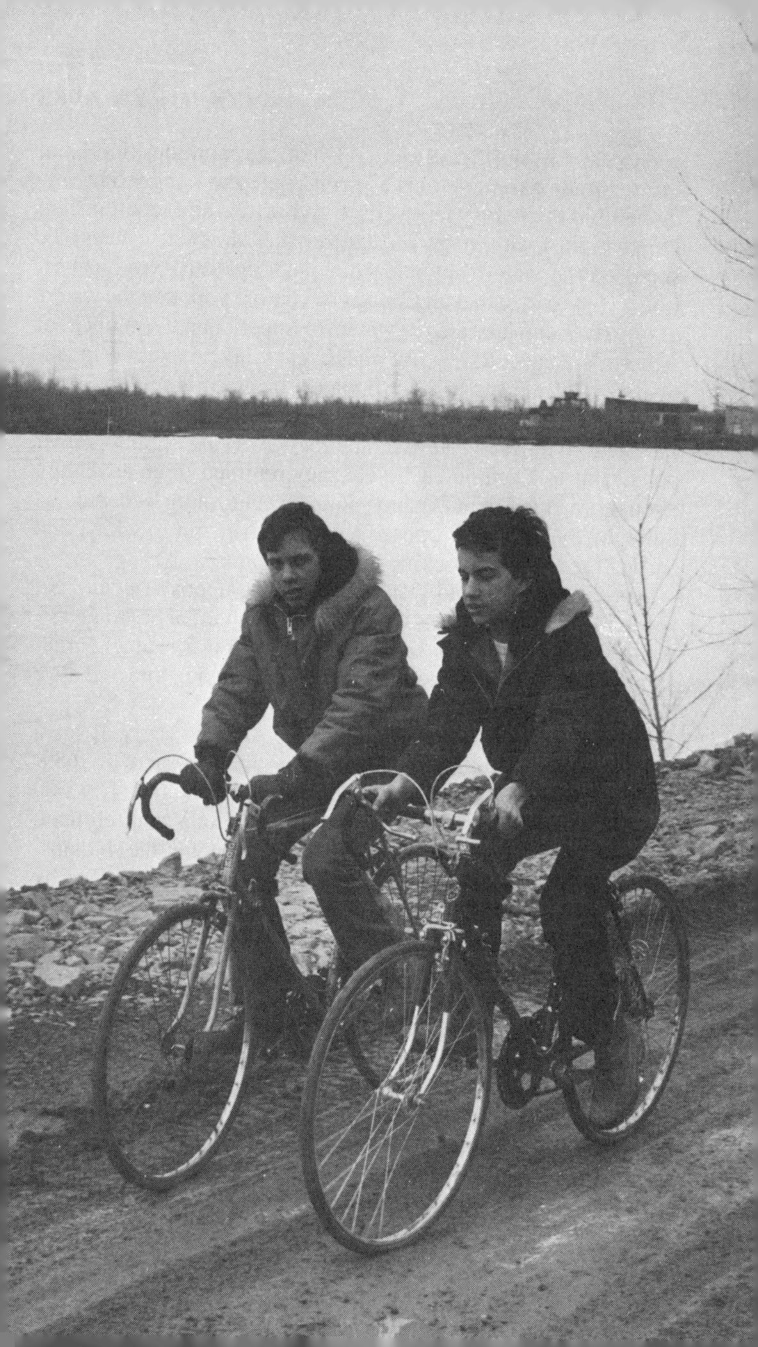

COUNTRY WALKS

and eventually absorbed. Here is where the enormous flotillas of the fur trade assembled each spring; here the swaggering *voyageurs* bid their noisy farewells to civilization and set off in their huge, eight-man *canots du maitre,* the Montreal canoes. To stand on the waterfront at Lachine and look out over Lake St. Louis is to realize that all Canada lies before you, that the waters of this river and lake are the waters of Superior and Winnipeg, of Alberta's Peace River and the Great Slave Lake — in all, one-third of the world's fresh water, much of it spilling down through forests of boreal spruce to form the broad highway of the St. Lawrence. From Lachine the *voyageurs* went to gather pelts, and to Lachine each year they returned in an adventure even more grand than that envisioned by the young Robert de La Salle, who in 1669 proposed that this river ran to China and earned the town its mocking name: La Chine.

Not far from the old warehouse, on the opposite side of St. Joseph Boulevard, stands the church and school of St. Anne. St. Anne was the patron of the *voyageurs,* and it was at an earlier church of the same name that they worshipped before and after their yearly expeditions.

On the wall outside the modern St. Anne's, you will see a plaque commemorating the terrible Lachine Massacre of 1689. Under cover of a hailstorm on the night of August 4, 1,500 Iroquois warriors paddled across Lake St. Louis and fell upon the village of Lachine. Part of the reason for the Indians' agitation was the recent seizure of some of their tribesmen by Governor Denonville, who had the captives carted off to slavery. But, whatever their grievances, the Iroquois who attacked Lachine were merciless. Men, women, and children were murdered in their beds, and their houses were burned down around them. Those who were captured alive were less fortunate — they were taken back to the south shore of the lake and roasted alive. Some were even eaten by the triumphant Iroquois. Throughout the latter part of the massacre, a French force of 300 men under the Marquis de Vaudreuil, which had been sent from Montreal by Denonville, stayed within a nearby fortification without ever seeking to engage the Iroquois in battle. Vaudreuil

PARC ANGRIGNON-LACHINE CANAL

believed himself to be carrying out orders to stay on the defensive — but for many of the hapless settlers at Lachine, the Marquis's conservative tactics may have meant the difference between life and death.

> *Turn right on any of the numbered avenues that end at St. Joseph Boulevard, and in two blocks you will come to Notre Dame Street, the main business thoroughfare of Lachine. There are several places here where you can get something to eat before heading back to the canal, or catching the Number 191 bus back to Montreal.*

The trails along the Lachine Canal are open to skiers every day from sunrise to 10 P.M. during January, February, and March, and to walkers and cyclists during the warmer months of the year. Please note, though, the above qualifications regarding warm weather access from Angrignon Park. For further information, call Parks Canada, 1156 Mill Street, Montreal, 514-932-8321 or 658-0681.

8

MAISONNEUVE PARK/ MONTREAL BOTANICAL GARDEN

Walking — ski touring in winter in Maisonneuve Park, adjacent to Botanical Garden grounds. During growing season, a beautifully varied outdoor display of trees, shrubs, flowers, herbs, ornamentals, and other plants; also, extensive indoor displays throughout the year.

THERE ARE TWO MAJOR PARKS in central Montreal. One, Mount Royal, is a natural preserve which largely represents the landscape vision of one man, Frederick Law Olmsted. The other, Maisonneuve, contains a beautifully conceived and constructed botanical garden which was the work of a Quebec native, Brother Marie-Victorin, E.C.

Brother Marie-Victorin, who is widely regarded as the greatest of all Canadian botanists (a postage stamp in his honor was issued in 1981), was a member of the faculty of the University of Montreal. Trained in the United States at Harvard, he nevertheless devoted much of his life to the study of the flora of his home province. Forty years of research and writing went into his masterwork, *Flore Laurentienne*, a comprehensive survey of the wild flora of southern Quebec and the Laurentian Mountains. The book is still published by the University of Montreal Press, and while knowledge of its subject has expanded, its scholarship has never been surpassed.

Throughout this busy career of teaching and writing, Brother Marie-Victorin still found time to pursue an old dream of his —

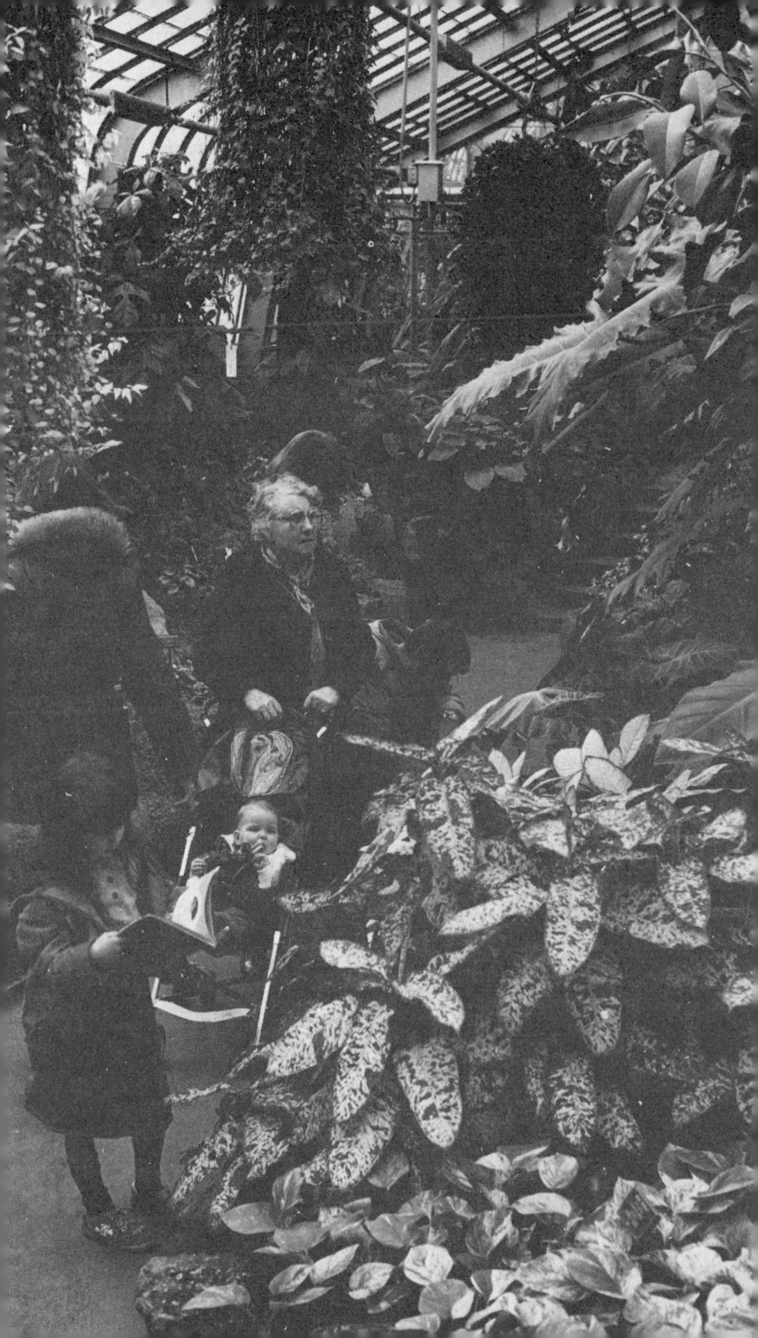

the establishment of a botanical garden which would serve as a showplace and educational resource for the public, and as a focus for scholarly research. With the support of well-placed friends such as Quebec Premier Maurice Duplessis and Montreal Mayor Camillien Houde, Marie-Victorin in 1931 received the governmental approval and financial commitments which enabled him to begin the project. But, planting and construction did not begin immediately. Five years passed while Marie-Victorin wrestled with the logistics of planning so large a garden, with the financial exigencies of the Great Depression, and — not the least of his worries — with political disputes that arose over the very nature of his ambitious proposal. A number of opposing voices simply questioned the wisdom of lavishing public funds on horticulture during a time of widespread poverty. Others, primarily anglophone residents of the west end, disapproved of locating the facility in the working class, overwhelmingly French precincts of east end Montreal. Even among Marie-Victorin's fellow faculty members at the university, there were those who felt that the garden was an unjustified priority.

With persistence, and some help from his political friends and supporters in the press, Marie-Victorin kept the project alive. One of the first steps he took during this planning period was an exceedingly wise one: he traveled to New York City and hired the brilliant landscape architect and horticulturist Henry Teuscher, then working at the Brooklyn Botanical Gardens. Teuscher designed the formal gardens, ponds, greenhouses, and nurseries at the new Montreal site, and stayed on as curator and chief horticulturist of the Garden until his retirement in 1962. Among his many accomplishments in this position was the development of outstanding orchid and bromeliad collections.

Along with the Botanical Garden, Brother Marie-Victorin founded the Botanical Institute of Montreal, an affiliate of the university at which he taught. He directed both the Institute and the Garden, which shared — and continue to share — office and research quarters at Maisonneuve Park. Marie-Victorin's study and teaching of botany, together with his close supervision of

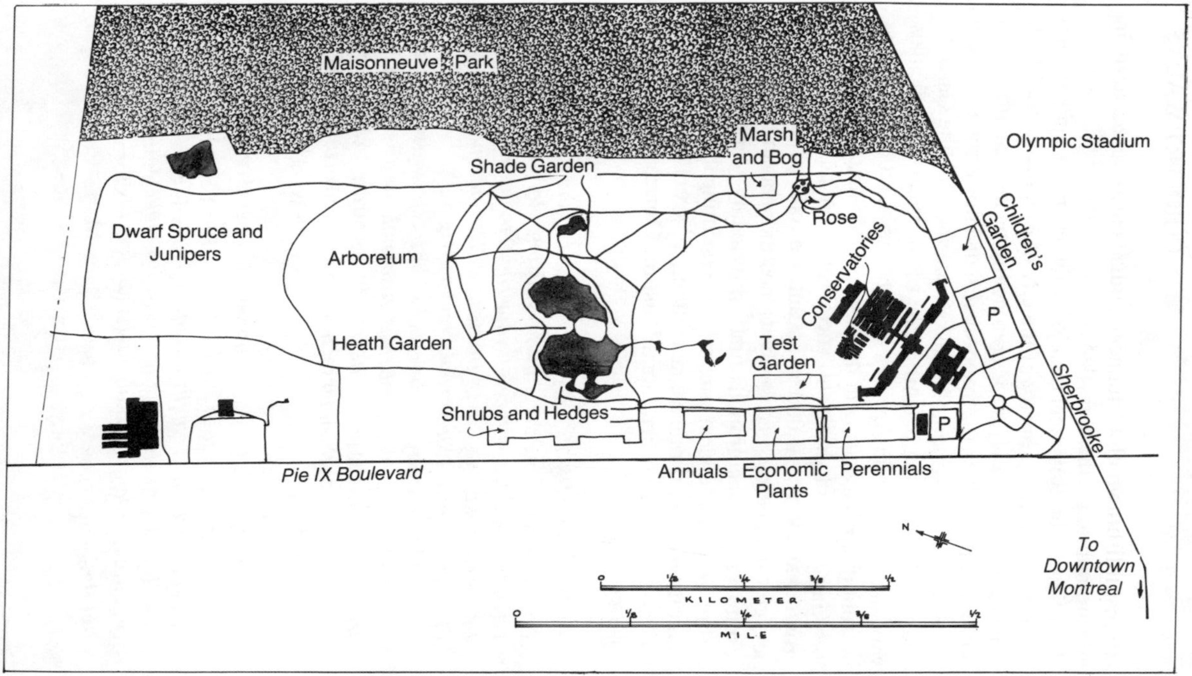
Maisonneuve Park
Olympic Stadium
Marsh and Bog
Shade Garden
Rose
Children's Garden
Dwarf Spruce and Junipers
Arboretum
Conservatories
P
Heath Garden
Test Garden
Sherbrooke
Shrubs and Hedges
P
Pie IX Boulevard
Annuals
Economic Plants
Perennials
N
To Downtown Montreal
0
1/8
1/4
3/8
1/2
KILOMETER
0
1/8
1/4
3/8
1/2
MILE

COUNTRY WALKS

the institutions which he founded, ended only with his death in an automobile accident in 1944.

Although the Botanical Garden is administered autonomously, it has been the property of the city of Montreal since 1940. One of its functions, as a community-owned facility, is to provide and maintain the trees, shrubs, and flowers which adorn the city's parks. Among the tasks undertaken by the Garden's administrators is the beautification of Montreal's 3,000 alleyways, and the planting of trees — at the rate of 8,000 per year — in front of each dwelling in the city. To accomplish these ends, the Garden maintains a 600-acre suburban nursery, with a growing stock of 150,000 trees. But, the focal point of all this horticultural energy, and surely its most extravagantly beautiful result, remains the grounds first cultivated by Marie-Victorin, Henry Teuscher, and an army of workers during the late 1930's. "Our mission is to bring nature to the city," says Pierre Bourque, the current chief horticulturist, "and the Garden is the heart of this mission."

PUBLIC TRANSIT: Take Metro Line 1 to the Pie IX station. Upon leaving the station, walk one block uphill (the Olympic Stadium will be on your right) to the intersection of Sherbrooke and Pie IX Boulevard. The entrance to the Garden is across Sherbrooke on your right.

The Garden may also be reached by bus from downtown Montreal. Take bus Number 24 eastbound on Sherbrooke, transferring at the end of the line (Bercy Street) to Number 185. Take 185 to the intersection of Sherbrooke and Pie IX Boulevard.

AUTOMOBILE: From downtown, drive east on Sherbrooke until you reach Pie IX Boulevard, which is the last street before the Olympic Stadium, looming just ahead on your left. Turn left onto Pie IX and then immediately right into the Garden's parking lot (small fee charged for parking).

MAISONNEUVE PARK

The Montreal Botanical Garden occupies 180 acres, comprising roughly half of Maisonneuve Park. (The remainder of the park — until several years ago a municipal golf course — is landscaped less for display than for strolling and relaxation, with trees, meadows, and picnic benches.) Within the Garden, nearly 25,000 plant species thrive within nine greenhouses and 30 separate yet well integrated areas, each of which represents a different botanical family, habitat group, or theme. Important indoor collections include over 1,200 species of orchids and 400 species of bromeliads, along with ferns, cacti, begonias, and gesneriads from around the world. Specific climatic regions are well represented: there are groupings of arid-climate and tropical plants; plants of Australia; and varieties cultivated primarily as houseplants.

A very recent addition to the indoor collections is the bonsai garden, which features specimens from the bonsai-like yet even more ancient Chinese pjenging tradition. The bonsai exhibit is built around a gift of 400 plantings from the Shanghai Botanical Garden and 200 from Japan — among which are 75 *satsuki* azaleas. The oldest bonsai in the new Montreal collection has been growing for 120 years.

The conservatories are also the locale of the Garden's seasonal cycle of exhibitions. From early November to mid-December, the main greenhouse is given over to a display of chrysanthemums. The Christmas displays, lavish with poinsettias, follow the mums and continue to mid-February. By the third week in March, the Easter exhibit has begun. This is the Garden's most extravagant production, and it sets the tone for the spring and summer. A particular theme — perhaps a tribute to a city or country — is chosen — and tulips, cherries, daffodils, rhododendrons, and azaleas run riot.

> *THE WALK: Having seen the indoor collections, visitors should obtain a map of the Garden so that they may best determine which paths to follow in order to see the plant groups in which they are most interested. Annuals are*

grouped along the walkway at the Sherbrooke/Pie IX entrance to the Garden. To the left of the conservatories, along Pie IX Boulevard, are perennials; plants of economic value; small fruits; the monastery and medicinal gardens; a collection of poisonous plants; a Quebec corner; and, shrubs and hedges. The vegetable test gardens, ground covers, alpinum, and mineralogical garden are behind the conservatories, while the children's garden is located on the opposite side of the buildings along Sherbrooke.

As you head past the ponds and flowery brook, the plantings become more expansive and the settings more deliberately naturalistic. The farthest reaches of the Garden are dominated by the arboretum, heath garden, and dwarf spruce and juniper collections. As you head back towards the conservatories along the border of Maisonneuve Park, don't miss the shade garden, marsh and bog plants, and rose collections.

No mention of the Montreal Botanical Gardens would be complete without reference to the Floralies International Exhibition, which occupies part of the former Expo '67 site on Ile Notre Dame in the St. Lawrence River. Floralies, like the Olympiad for which Montreal played host in 1976, is a recurring event in which many nations participate; it is sanctioned by the International Association of Horticultural Producers and the International Bureau of Exhibitions. Montreal's turn to stage this floral extravaganza came in 1980; however, the Ile Notre Dame setting continues to bloom with a permanent horticultural show in which, as of this writing, 13 nations and several regions of Canada are participating. The original organization and continuing maintenance of Floralies have been the responsibility of the Montreal Botanical Garden. Of its variety, chief horticulturist Pierre Bourque remarks that "we now have a representation of every major landscape architecture tradition in the world."

MAISONNEUVE PARK

To get to Floralies from downtown Montreal, take Metro Line 4 to the Ile Ste. Helene station, and walk across the Pont du Cosmos (bridge) to Ile Notre Dame. Or, take bus Number 168 from Peel station, on Metro Line 1.

Montreal Botanical Garden, 4101 East Sherbrooke Street, Montreal H1X 2B2, is open daily throughout the year. For information, call 514-872-2647 or 514-872-4543.

9

ILE DES MOULINS—TERREBONNE

Walking — 1 mile on island; also walks in the adjoining town of Terrebonne. A restoration of the office and mills belonging to an historic seigneurial estate on the Riviere des Mille Iles.

TERREBONNE IS A SMALL TOWN on the north shore of the Riviere des Mille Iles, one of the two arms of the Ottawa that encircle Ile Jesus and the city of Laval. With its old churches and narrow streets, it resembles many of the other settlements that dot the landscape between the St. Lawrence lowlands and the Laurentians. But, Terrebonne is fortunate in having had preserved — formerly by accident, and more recently by design — a significant portion of its early history. This heritage takes the form of the stone mills and administrative buildings of the old seigneury of Terrebonne, which stand on the Ile des Moulins, and have been restored by the Quebec Ministry of Cultural Affairs.

> *PUBLIC TRANSIT: Buses between Montreal and Terrebonne are operated by Transport de Laval. They leave Montreal from the Henri Bourassa station (last northbound stop on Metro Line 2), and arrive in Terrebonne at the Richard Restaurant on the corner of Rue St. Pierre and Rue St. Andre. The Ile des Moulins causeway is three blocks west of this point, at the end of St. Pierre.*

Ile des Moulins: the New Mill

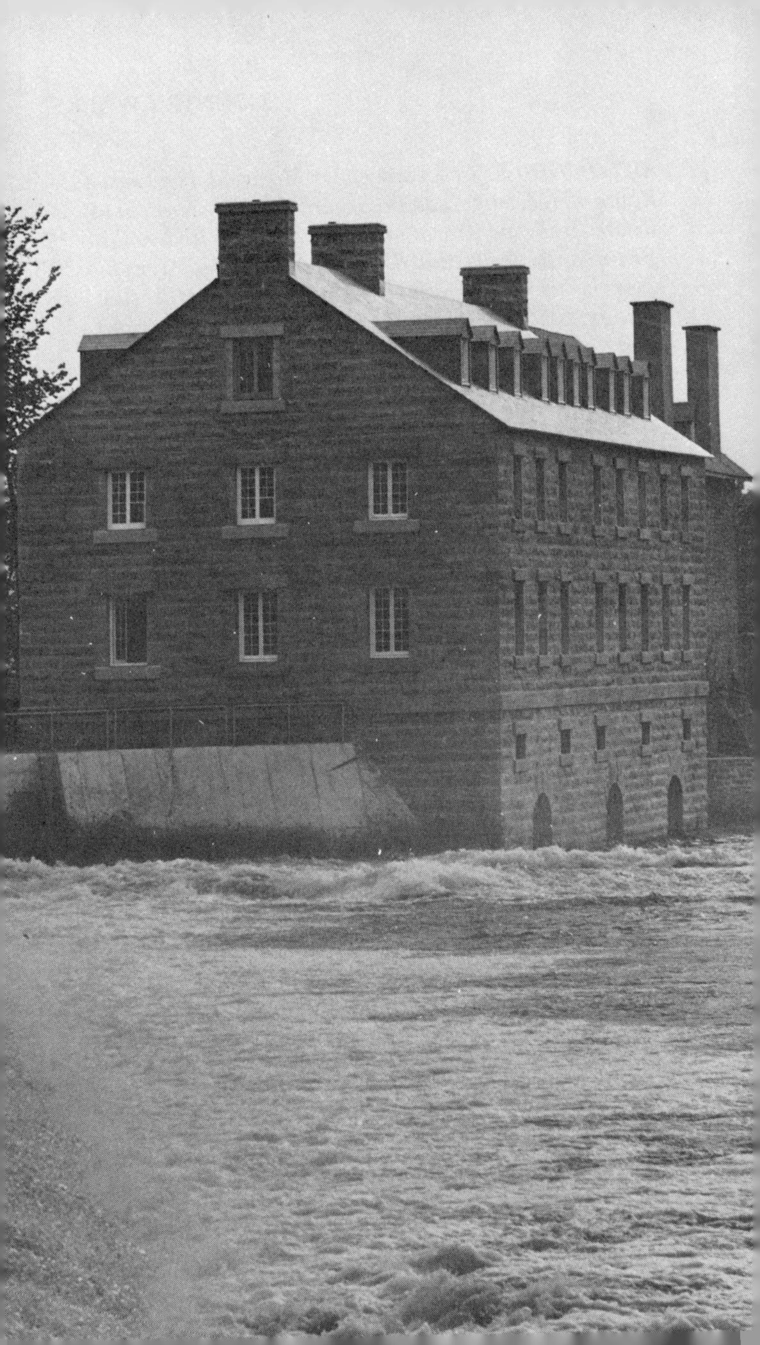

COUNTRY WALKS

AUTOMOBILE: From downtown Montreal, head east on Route 40 (Metropolitan Boulevard), turning north onto Route 25. Route 25 will take you across the Riviere des Prairies, Ile Jesus, and Riviere des Mille Iles. Signs for Terrebonne appear just after the Riviere des Mille Iles bridge. Exit onto Route 125 (Boulevard des Seigneurs), and turn right onto Rue Moody at the first intersection. After 1 block, turn left onto Rue St. Louis and continue along the river for approximately ¾ mile. Turn right onto Boulevard des Braves. Parking for the Ile des Moulins is 2 blocks farther on your left.

The words "seigneury," "seigneurial", and "seigneur" appear and reappear in this book, perhaps to the puzzlement of readers unfamiliar with the history of French Canada. So much evidence of the old seigneurial days remains on the Ile des Moulins that perhaps here is the best place to look into the workings of what Samuel Eliot Morison has called "the most successful feudal land settlement scheme in all North America."

It is difficult for us to imagine how vast New France must have seemed to the people who first undertook its settlement and administration. Their native country extended no more than six hundred miles in any direction; yet, a voyage of that distance was required just to get from the island of Anticosti, in the Gulf of St. Lawrence, to the place where Montreal was built. A fur trader paddling from Montreal to the western tip of Lake Erie, near La Mothe Cadillac's outpost of Detroit, would have covered no more territory if he had traveled from Paris to Marseille. No wonder the pioneers consoled themselves with the thought that China was somewhere out near Minneapolis; no wonder their hearts sank when they tasted fresh water in Lake Superior.

To colonize such a place as New France would require more than a haphazard effort. France's solution — first put into practice in the 1620's, during the governorship of Samuel de

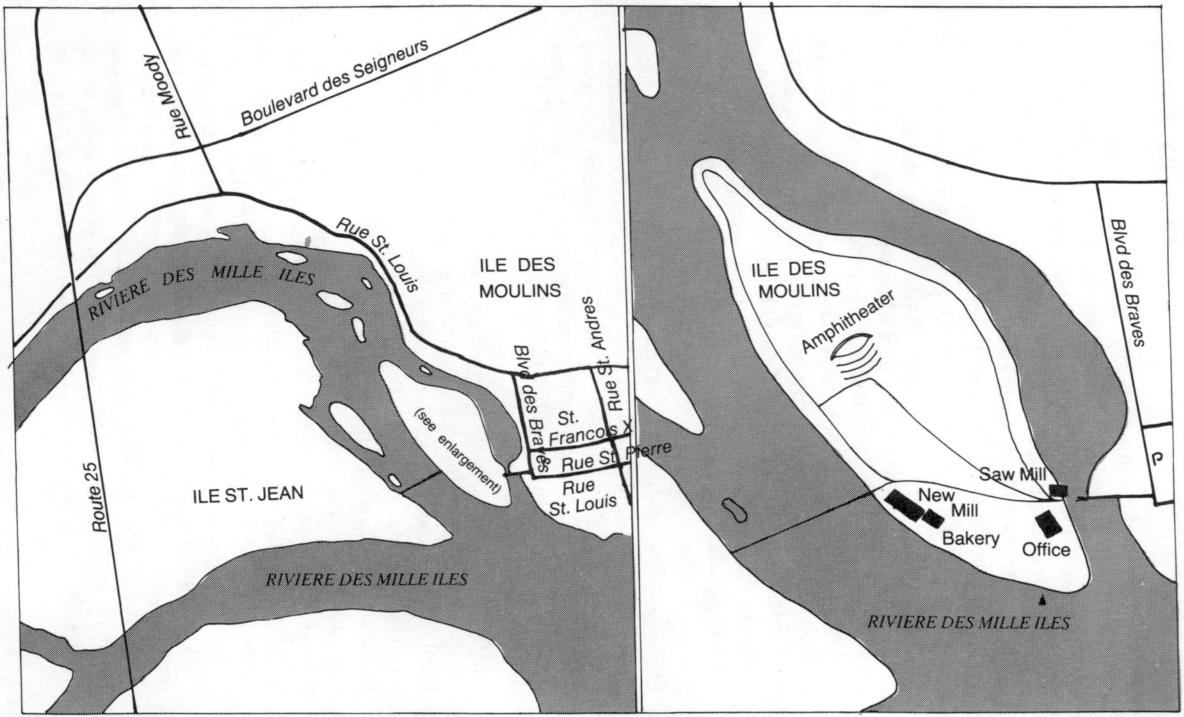

Boulevard des Seigneurs
Rue Moody
Rue St. Louis
ILE DES MOULINS
RIVIERE DES MILLE ILES
Blvd des Braves
Rue St. Andres
St. Francois X
Rue St. Pierre
Rue St. Louis
(see enlargement)
Route 25
ILE ST. JEAN
RIVIERE DES MILLE ILES
ILE DES MOULINS
Amphitheater
Blvd des Braves
P
Saw Mill
New Mill
Bakery
Office
RIVIERE DES MILLE ILES

COUNTRY WALKS

Champlain, and resumed later in the century on a much larger scale — was a species of feudalism uniquely adapted to the conditions of the wilderness. It involved the granting of fiefdoms, called seigneuries, to individuals who would promise to clear the forests and sub-grant farmland to colonists.

The feudal arrangements of French Canada bore little resemblance to the system of vassalage and serfdom that we associate with the Middle Ages. For one thing, the seigneurs were not always wealthy, and they often worked just as hard as their titular inferiors, the small farmers or *habitants*. As for the *habitants* themselves, their responsibilities to the seigneur extended no further than the cultivation of their land, the use of the seigneurial mill for grinding their grain, and the payment of a nominal rent. Occasionally, they might also be required to contribute a few days' labor to the upkeep of the estate.

New France was thus provided with a convenient hierarchy: king, governor, seigneurs, and *habitants*. (Occasionally, there would be an extra tier of authority. On the Island of Montreal, for instance, the Gentlemen of St. Sulpice frequently carved smaller seigneuries from their enormous holdings.) The system generally worked quite well, serving the legal, agricultural, and defense needs of the colony.

Terrebonne was one such seigneury, although at first, not one of the most successful. It was granted in 1673 to Sieur Andre Daulier des Landes, a gentleman who never took the trouble to cross the Atlantic and see it. This absentee seigneur sold his title to Louis Le Comte Dupre, who evidently was no more conscientious than his predecessor in meeting the landholder's traditional obligations. These included provision of facilities for grinding grain; yet, in 1707, we find the local settlers securing permission to set up their own water-powered mill.

In 1718, a priest named Louis Lepage became the first resident seigneur of Terrebonne. Lepage was truly interested in the improvement of the property. He built a stone causeway to connect Ile des Moulins with the mainland, and constructed water-powered flour and saw mills upon it. (The island's name must date from his tenure, as "moulins" means "mills" in

ILE DES MOULINS — TERREBONNE

French.) Lepage's legacy also included the first manor house and Terrebonne's first church.

Terrebonne prospered under Lepage and his successor, Sieur de Lacorne, who paid 60,000 French pounds for the property in 1745. The line of French seigneurs came to an end, though, in 1784. By that time, the British had held Canada for a quarter century, and a new breed of energetic Scottish merchants were consolidating their economic power in the Montreal area. One of them, Joseph Jordan, became seigneur of Terrebonne. In 1802, he was followed by Simon McTavish, the richest man in Montreal. McTavish was a partner in the North West Company, and was the builder of the Mt. Royal mansion (Chapter 10), which long stood unfinished and empty after his death. Like Terrebonne's earliest seigneurs, McTavish too was an absentee landlord, but he left far more of a mark on the town — particularly on the Ile des Moulins. He built the 1803 bakery, which still stands, as well as new flour and saw mills. It was during the McTavish era that industry joined agriculture as a mainstay of the local economy. The Scot established fulling and carding mills, along with housing for the new textile workers. By the early nineteenth century, the old purposes of land clearing and colonization had long been met, and the commercial prerogatives of an ambitious seigneur had broadened.

McTavish was succeeded by his old fur-trading associate Roderick McKenzie, a cousin of Alexander MacKenzie (he spelled the Scottish prefix differently), the first man to reach the Pacific Ocean via a Canadian overland route. In his manor at Terrebonne, Roderick McKenzie often played host to visiting western traders, and many of the "factors" — the middle management of the fur outposts — sent their children here for schooling. The seigneur also entertained the American writer Washington Irving, who had come to Terrebonne to gather material for his fur trade chronicle, *Astoria*.

The last great seigneurial name to be associated with Terrebonne and the Ile des Moulins was that of Joseph Masson and his wife, Genevieve-Sophie Raymond, who held sway between 1832 and the technical abolition of the old system in 1854.

COUNTRY WALKS

The Massons were responsible for the final spate of construction on the Ile des Moulins, and it is in large part their legacy that survives today. The handsome stone saw and flour mills were built just before Joseph Masson's death in 1847, as was the seigneurial office, which now houses the new historical interpretation center. Masson's widow supervised the completion of the New Mill and the manor house on Rue St. Louis, just north of the Ile des Moulins.

Madame Masson died in 1883. Terrebonne's importance as a mill town did not long outlive her; after the turn of the century, more and more of the sturdy old structures on the Ile des Moulins fell vacant, or were altered to meet the needs of petty entrepreneurs. Some were simply used for storage. By 1967, part of the island had been sectioned into lots for mobile homes, and the seigneurial office was an apartment house. The bakery and New Mill were obscured by a fish market. Little thought was given to the historical significance of this fine, beautifully integrated complex of buildings.

The tide turned in 1974, when Quebec's Ministry of Cultural Affairs expropriated the Ile des Moulins. The bold plans which the ministry announced have taken nearly a decade to realize, but the island today is well on its way towards becoming the cultural and historical resource originally envisioned when the expropriation was made.

THE WALK: The Ile des Moulins is joined to the mainland by a short causeway leading from the parking area on Boulevard des Braves, Terrebonne. Cross the causeway and walk along the row of restored buildings on your left. From here, you may make a complete circuit of the small, lozenge-shaped island, or you may turn left at the New Mill onto a pedestrian walkway extending atop the impoundment which holds back the waters of the Riviere des Mille Iles. This is the dam which once harnessed power for the old seigneury's various milling and manufacturing operations. It connects the Ile des Moulins with a small park on Ile St. Jean. This stretch of the Riviere des Mille Iles is

Dam across the Riviere des Mille Iles

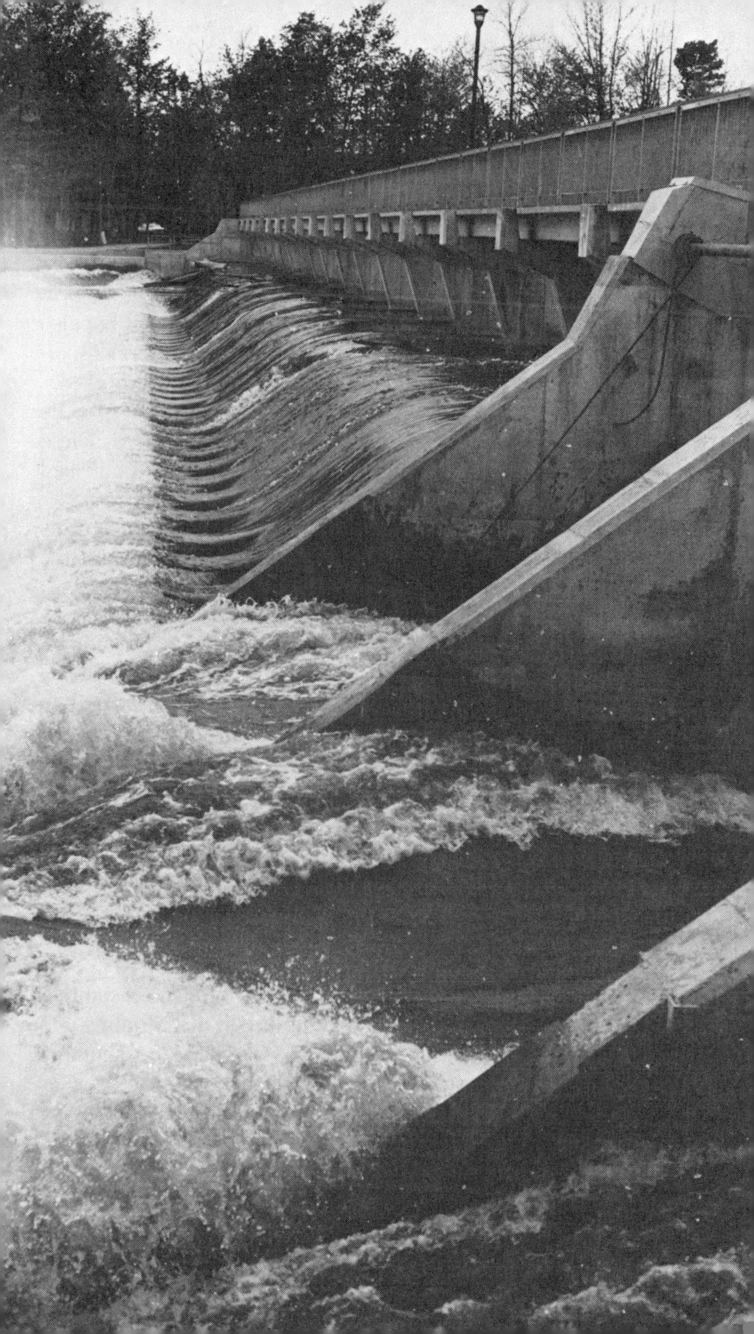

COUNTRY WALKS

regularly stocked with trout, and it is possible to fish both above and below the dam.

The building immediately on your left, after you cross the causeway from the parking area, is the seigneurial office of the late 1840's. This was one of the first of the island's buildings to be restored. It houses not only the interpretation center but also the headquarters of the Terrebonne Historical society. The society has recently been engaged in recording interviews with older residents of Terrebonne, including some who remember the Ile des Moulins when the mills were still in operation. These interviews will be incorporated into a soon-to-be-published history of the area.

Visitors to the old seigneurial office should take notice of its plank floors and interior woodwork, all fine examples of the Quebec country vernacular.

Just opposite the office is the 1804 sawmill, which now houses the island's special library collections. Farther down along the river, on the left, is the bakery, also a relic of the McTavish days. The restored structure's stone ovens are still in place. The last of the major buildings along the shore of the Riviere des Mille Iles — and the largest — is Madame Masson's New Mill, which has been refurbished and transformed into a cultural center.

If you continue walking towards the northern end of the island, rather than turning onto the dam, you will cross a 12-acre park and come to a small outdoor theater. A repertory of plays, mostly with Quebec folkloric themes, is presented here in summer.

Guided tours are also part of the Culture Ministry's summer program. These walks extend beyond the Ile des Moulins into the old neighborhoods of Terrebonne, where there are a number of historic colonial structures. Among them are the Jacques Perra, Pierre Auger, and Noel Roussille houses. A map showing the location of these and other local points of interest is posted on the ground floor of the seigneurial office at the Ile des Moulins.

ILE DES MOULINS — TERREBONNE

Absorbing all this history can make you hungry. There are two interesting restaurants within a short walk of the Ile des Moulins. Phidimus, a half block from Boulevard des Braves on Rue Francis Xavier, serves traditional Quebecois fare. La Auberge de La Cote, at the corner of Boulevard des Braves and Rue St. Louis (see automobile directions, above), is somewhat more formal, with a spectacular fixed-price menu which includes selected wines.

Ile des Moulins, Terrebonne, Quebec, is administered by the province's Ministry of Cultural Affairs. For information on hours when buildings are open, summer theater, and guided tours, call 514-471-2122.

10

MOUNT ST. HILAIRE NATURE CONSERVATION CENTER

Walking, ski touring, and snowshoeing — 15 miles of trails traversing a 1,500-acre preserve on Mt. St. Hilaire, one of the Monteregian hills that rises to the east of Montreal. Despite hundreds of years of settlement on the surrounding plain, the center's property has remained a virtual wilderness.

STAND ATOP PAIN DE SUCRE on a clear winter morning, and look down upon the lowlands of the St. Lawrence. The plain through which the great river flows appears to be a vast lake of snow, from which rise the islands of the Monteregian hills. There, to the west, is Mt. Bruno; farther to the north stands Mt. Royal, with the skyscrapers of Montreal clustered around its base. The Monteregians, indeed, once were islands, with the waters of the Champlain Sea lapping at their slopes.

Near the foot of Mt. St. Hilaire, the Richelieu River flows northward towards its meeting with the St. Lawrence at Sorel. To the French settlers of the seventeenth century, the Richelieu was the River of Death, for it was the highway used by the Iroquois when they staged their murderous raids. Because of the Indian threat, the Eastern Townships — that part of Quebec roughly defined by the Richelieu and St. Lawrence rivers and the western boundary of Maine — was among the last regions of New France to be settled and farmed. It was not until 1694 that Jean-Baptiste Hertel petitioned the colony's Intendant for the

Mount St. Hilaire: Lac Hertel in winter

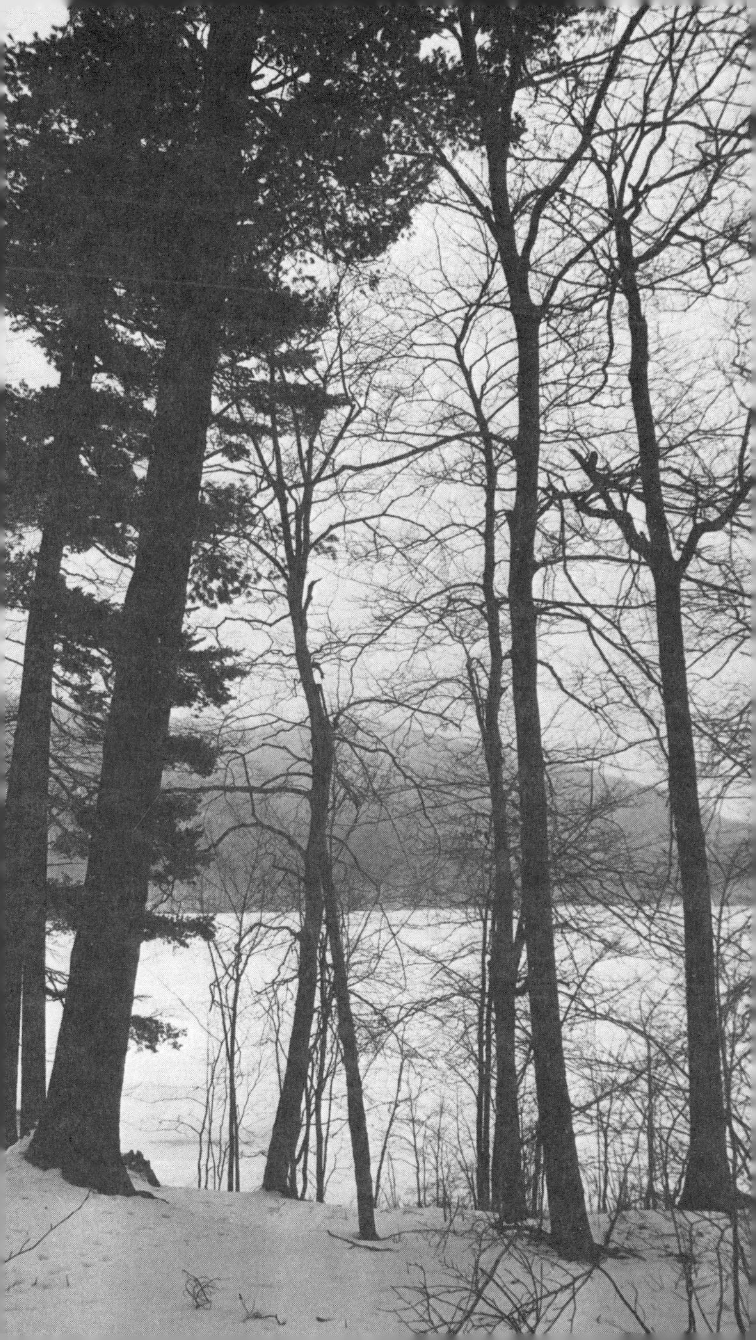

seigneury of Rouville, which included Mt. St. Hilaire. The property remained in the Hertel family for 150 years.

Jean-Baptiste Hertel's original grant covered over 35,000 acres, an area far larger than the present Conservation Center. It included ample river frontage, as well as much of the farmland which, when you look from the top of Pain de Sucre, you see spreading towards the Richelieu. The first seigneur of Rouville cleared very little of this land, but during the tenure of his son, Jean-Baptiste Francois Hertel, twenty riverside farms were carved from the property and granted to *habitants* according to the traditional feudal arrangement. The mountain played very little part in this agricultural development, other than as a watershed for the stream which powered the seigneury's mill. There was timber aplenty on the lower, more accessible stretches of the domain, so few trees were felled on the higher slopes.

In 1844, the last seigneur of Rouville sold his land to the Campbell family, who kept it for three generations. During all this time, the "accidental" preservation of Mt. St. Hilaire continued. In 1912, that portion of the old seigneury which includes the mountain was purchased by Brigadier A. Hamilton Gault. Gault was an avid conservationist, who during his lifetime arranged the eventual bequest of his 2,700-acre estate to McGill University. In 1958, shortly after completing the handsome lodge that overlooks Lake Hertel, Gault died, and the University accepted stewardship of Mt. St. Hilaire. By then, the mountain's slopes comprised one of the only tracts of residual mature forest — uncut and unmanaged — remaining in the Montreal area. These woods look much the same as they did to the first Quebecois, and to their Iroquois nemeses.

In order to keep it that way, and to help McGill manage its mountain property both for research and recreation, the private, non-profit Mount St. Hilaire Nature Conservation Center was established in 1972. Membership in the Center is available through the payment of a modest annual fee; non-members are charged for parking on weekends. The Center is always free to pedestrians.

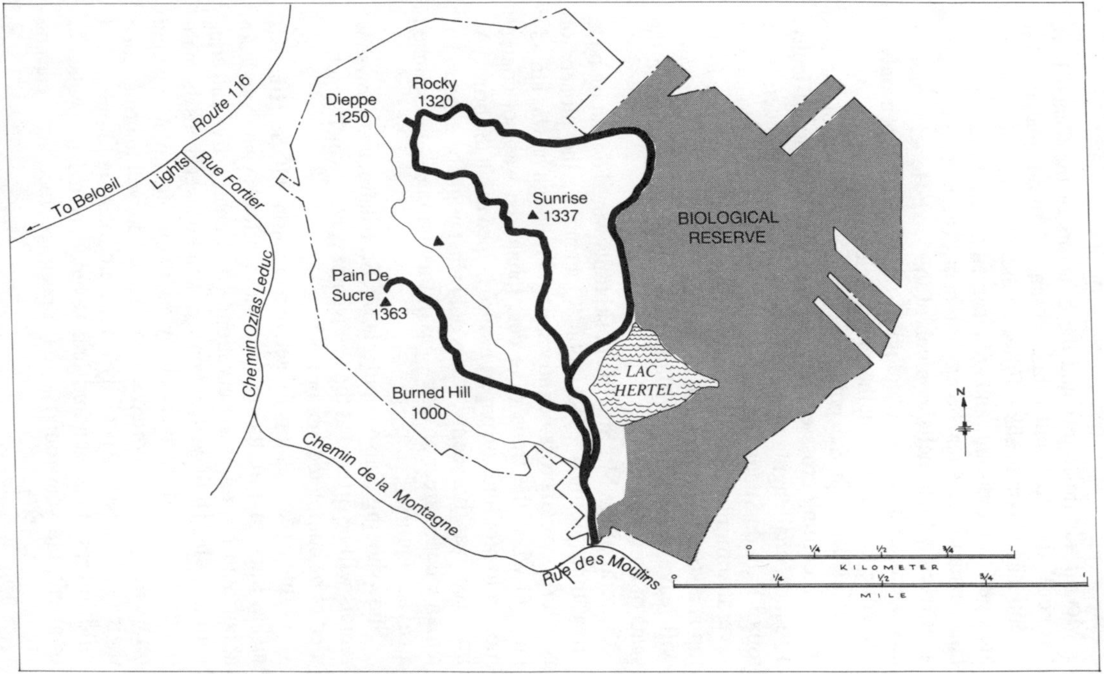

Route 116
To Beloeil
Lights
Rue Fortier
Chemin Ozias Leduc
Chemin de la Montagne
Rue des Moulins
Dieppe
1250
Rocky
1320
Sunrise
1337
Pain De
Sucre
1363
Burned Hill
1000
BIOLOGICAL
RESERVE
LAC
HERTEL
N
0
1/4
1/2
3/4
1
KILOMETER
MILE

COUNTRY WALKS

McGill administrators and the directors of the Center have "zoned" the old Gault estate so that it can adequately serve scientist and layman alike. Fifteen hundred acres of the property are open to the public, and are reserved for activities which do not substantially alter the environment. The remaining 1,200-acre tract, which includes much of the Lake Hertel shoreline, has been set aside as a biological reserve. It is open only to accredited researchers in the natural sciences.

Lacing through the public sector are 15 miles of marked trails, including cross-country ski routes of varying difficulty. The most challenging of these is the trail which meanders to the top of Pain de Sucre, the highest (1,363 feet) of the mountain's several summits. It's only fair to point out that the route to the top is also the route back to the bottom, and that it is one which will leave most skiers wishing they had foam padding in the seats of their knickers.

Several of the Mt. St. Hilaire ski trails were laid out by none other than Herman "Jackrabbit" Johannsen, the pioneer of North American cross-country skiing. Although he was already past 90 when the trails were cut, Johannsen was not content merely to plot lines on paper: he also helped to cut the brush. As impressive as this seems, it was only what might be expected of a man whose career on skis — as of this writing — has spanned an even century.

Snowshoeing is also popular at Mt. St. Hilaire, and snowshoe rentals will be offered at the new visitor center, which is scheduled to be completed late in 1982.

As fine a place as it is for active recreation, Mt. St. Hilaire is just as important for the opportunities it affords visitors to learn about nature through observation. The Center's five full-time naturalists lead bilingual interpretive walks on weekends throughout the year, and are available by reservation for groups visiting on weekdays. Unescorted walkers would do well to bring along their field guides, especially if they are interested in birds and wildflowers. One hundred and seventy-six avian species — transient and year-round — have been recorded here, earning

MOUNT ST. HILAIRE NATURE CENTER

Mt. St. Hilaire the status of a federal sanctuary. The Center's botanical endowments are no less superb. Not counting mosses and lichens, there are nearly 600 species of plants living on the mountain. A gorgeous display of wildflowers begins each May, and lasts through much of the year.

Several of Mt. St. Hilaire's plants are extremely rare — at least in this portion of their range. One is *Potentilla tridentata*, which was among the first flowering plants to appear after the last continental glaciers receded. It is usually found only in the Arctic, or along exposed stretches of northern seacoast, but it survives in rock crevices on the exposed peak of Pain de Sucre. Here, the little plant finds a microclimate in which favorable conditions prevail. *Potentilla tridentata* produces white flowers in summer, and in fall its leaves turn rust-colored. You'll have to look closely for it. Natural selection has assured its survival not only by adapting it to a harsh climate, but by tucking it into crannies where it is safe from the tread of humans and animals. By all means, leave *Potentilla* where you find it and resist the temptation to pick any other wildflowers growing at Mt. St. Hilaire. Collecting of plant materials is strictly prohibited by the Center.

Mt. St. Hilaire is also well-known for its distinctive geological composition. Like the other Monteregian hills, it represents a magmatic intrusion into a layer of sediment. (A more thorough discussion of the formation of the Monteregians can be found in Chapter 3.) The material of the Mt. St. Hilaire intrusion is largely syenite and essexite. Within the syenite is found a breccia zone, incorporating fragments of hornfels, marble, and essexite which cooled and "froze" within the syenite after the latter substance made its way into the pre-existing essexite and sedimentary formations.

Many of the more than 100 mineral species found at Mt. St. Hilaire are known in few other localities in the world. At least three new forms of serandite crystals have been discovered, and a surprising number of rare silicates have turned up. The "contact zones," where the hot magma met with the local limestone

COUNTRY WALKS

sediment, have yielded a considerable variety of species.

PUBLIC TRANSIT: The closest any bus comes to the Mt. St. Hilaire Nature Conservation Center is the intersection of Route 116, the St. Hyacinthe Road, with Rue Fortier in the town of Mt. St. Hilaire. Access to the center from this point involves a 3½-mile uphill walk along the route described below for motorists. Bus travel to Mt. St. Hilaire is therefore not recommended.

AUTOMOBILE: Leave Montreal via the Victoria Bridge and follow the signs for Route 116. Follow Route 116 through the towns of St. Hubert and Beloeil. Just after the road bridges the Richelieu River, it enters the town of Mt. St. Hilaire. Approximately ½ mile past the bridge, turn right at the traffic light onto Rue Fortier. Follow Rue Fortier 2/3 mile until it merges with Chemin Ozias Leduc. Proceed directly ahead on Ozias Leduc for approximately 1 mile, and turn left onto Chemin de la Montagne. After another 1½ miles, continue directly ahead onto Rue des Moulins. The center gate is 300 yards farther, on the left.

THE WALK: Trails lead from the parking lot and visitor center to Lake Hertel and to the five summits of Mt. St. Hilaire which lie within the Center's public sector. These are: Dieppe (1,250 feet, with cliffs descending to the west); Rocky (1,320 feet); Sunrise (1,337 feet); Pain de Sucre (1,363 feet); and, Burned Hill (1,000 feet). All trail markings are color-coded. For a pleasant circuit which offers a complete sampling of the Center's varied terrain, follow the red-blazed trail which skirts the shore of Lake Hertel and the boundary of the biological reserve. Return via the blue trail which links Rocky and Sunrise summits and rejoins the red trail near the lake (total distance approximately 5 miles). The above-mentioned Pain de Sucre trail (yellow-blazed) is also recommended, either in ski season or summer. Maps are available at the visitor center.

MOUNT ST. HILAIRE NATURE CENTER

The Mt. St. Hilaire Nature Conservation Center, 422 Rue des Moulins, is open all year. Hours vary with the season; opening is always at 8 A.M., and closing at about dusk. Camping, fires, barbecues, horseback riding, and pets are prohibited, as are all vehicles — including bicycles — beyond the parking lot. Groups of more than 10 should reserve well in advance by telephone. For information, call 514-467-1755.

11

COTE ST. CATHERINE PARK/ ST. LAWRENCE SEAWAY

Walking and cycling — a park on the south shore of the St. Lawrence River, separated from the mainland by the St. Lawrence Seaway. From the park, an 8½-mile bicycle path extends along the Seaway to Nun's Island and the Victoria Bridge.

THE LACHINE CANAL COULDN'T DO THE JOB forever. Even though this engineering marvel of the 1820's (see Chapter 7) had been enlarged and linked, by the turn of the century, with a 14-foot-deep system of canals affording access from the Atlantic to Lake Superior, the size of modern ships and the volume of modern shipping clearly demanded an entirely new waterway. The Canadians knew it, and the Americans knew it — all that remained was to draw plans along politically and fiscally equitable lines, and to overcome (or defuse) the opposition of those interests which had a stake in the continuing difficulty of inland navigation in North America — chiefly American railways and the coast cities.

All that remained, indeed. Between the first serious realization of the need for an improved ship channel along the St. Lawrence and the breaking of ground for the Seaway, a span of some 60 years intervened. Throughout this time, it was the Canadians who pressed the need for the Seaway with greater force, while voices in the United States raised reservation after reservation. It is difficult in the 1980's to think of American

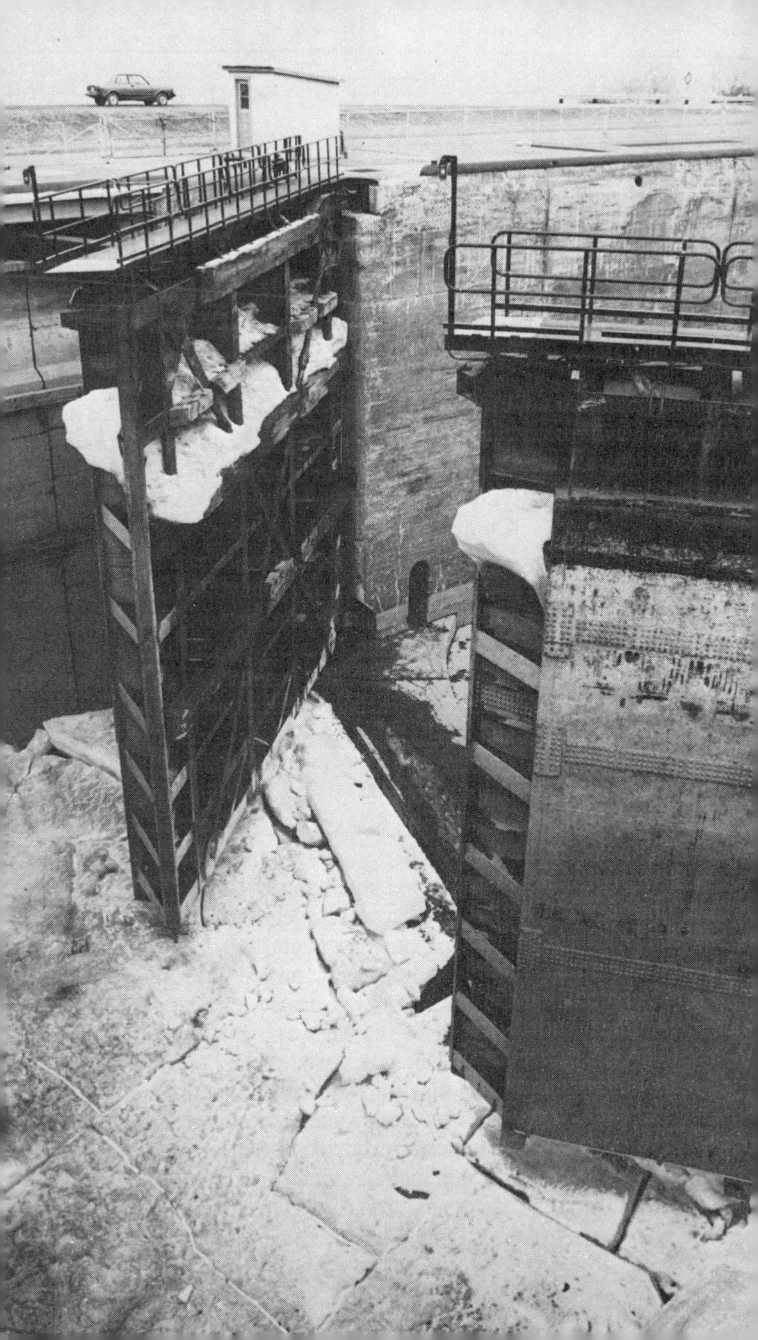

railways as capable of carrying that much political clout; but, in the prewar years they were a force to be reckoned with, and any threat to their freight revenues — whether real or imagined — was not taken lightly. Seaports such as New York and Philadelphia reacted similarly, as they envisioned tonnage which might otherwise have been loaded or unloaded at their docks instead finding its way in and out of upstart harbors in the hinterlands. It seemed, to put it simply, as if the coast were being moved. And, in a sense it was: writing about the project in his book *The St. Lawrence Seaway,* Lionel Chevrier concluded that "the Seaway has given Canada a south coast stretching half-way across the nation." Yet, in his enthusiasm for the Seaway (he served as president of the authority which supervised its construction), Chevrier allowed himself a prediction which could have bolstered the worst fears of the Easterners. The new waterway, he said, would allow Montreal, Toronto, and Chicago to "become as large as New York." In the quarter century that has passed since those words were written, that prophecy has of course not been fulfilled — as much to the relief of prudent urban planners in Montreal, Toronto, and Chicago as to the boosters of New York. What the Seaway *has* done, and done quite efficiently, is to enable ocean-going vessels to move commodities such as midwestern grain into world markets, and to carry raw materials (particularly Labrador iron ore) to the manufacturing cities along the Great Lakes.

By 1941, Canada and the United States had agreed in principle to proceed with the Seaway project. But, World War II intervened, and it was not until the beginning of the 1950's that the attention of the two nations again turned seriously to the St. Lawrence. By then, Canada was nearly as interested in the hydroelectric byproduct of the Seaway's construction as she was in the shipping advantages it would offer, and the United States got the message that unless resistance south of the border was overcome, the Canadians would take on the entire project themselves. This suggestion did the trick; congressional approval was given to American participation early in 1954, and by that summer the construction crews were on the job.

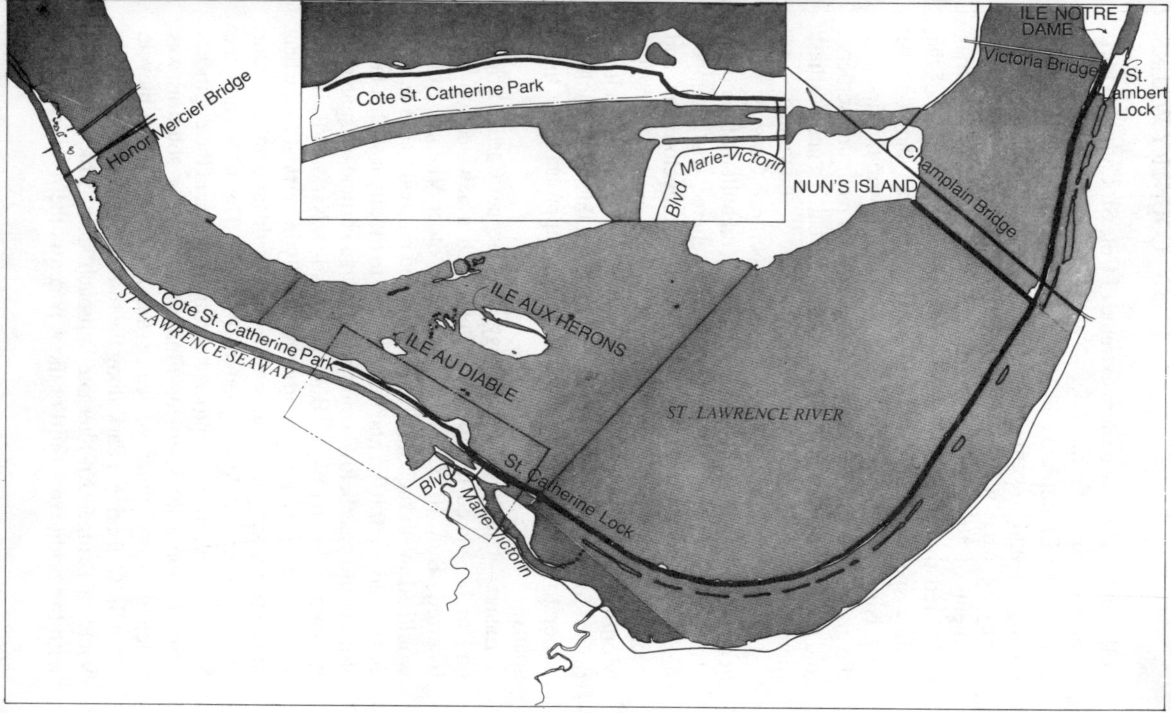
Cote St. Catherine Park
Blvd Marie-Victorin
ILE NOTRE DAME
Victoria Bridge
St. Lambert Lock
NUN'S ISLAND
Champlain Bridge
Honor Mercier Bridge
Cote St. Catherine Park
ST. LAWRENCE SEAWAY
ILE AUX HERONS
ILE AU DIABLE
ST. LAWRENCE RIVER
St. Catherine Lock
Blvd Marie-Victorin

COUNTRY WALKS

If you stand at the eastern extreme of Cote St. Catherine Park — near the St. Catherine Lock — and look along the south shore towards the Champlain and Victoria Bridges, then back across the rapids and towards the Honore Mercier Bridge, you are surveying what was by far the most challenging and costly segment of this vast construction project. Lionel Chevrier estimated that the Lachine section absorbed half of all of the money spent to build the Seaway. Perhaps this shouldn't be surprising — the rapids of Lachine, after all, were the first and the greatest barrier to navigation which faced incoming settlers, and the Lachine Canal itself was one of the earliest and costliest measures taken to facilitate shipping on the St. Lawrence.

Like the Lachine Canal, the St. Lawrence Seaway was, according to the original plans, to have been built on the northern, Montreal side of the river. This scheme was scrapped because of the density of the city's waterfront development, and because of the swiftness of the St. Mary's current along the Montreal shore. Also, Seaway construction required the alteration of four major bridges, and it was felt that this work would be easier to accomplish at the south shore approaches to these spans.

Easier — but by no means easy. The Jacques Cartier Bridge had to be jacked up 50 feet, after which a new section was inserted. But, 10,000 feet upriver, the older Victoria Bridge would allow no such flexibility. It carried railroad tracks as well as automobile traffic, and the only way to modify it so that large ships could pass below would be to insert a vertical lift span near its south shore terminus. But, the Canadian National Railroad, which owned the bridge, protested loudly: a vertical lift, when raised to accommodate Seaway traffic, would hold up rush-hour trains for an intolerable length of time. The C.N. and the Seaway Authority got into a shouting match, and the engineers were temporarily stymied. Finally, though, a solution was reached — one which you can examine close up if you bicycle from St. Catherine's Park along the route described below to the Victoria Bridge. An alternate approach span, which connects with the bridge one-third of the way across the river, was built

COTE ST. CATHERINE PARK

across the Seaway bed. Vertical lift spans were installed in both branches of the redesigned bridge. A lock was placed beneath the original bridge approach. When a ship approaches the lock — in this example from the east — the first lift is raised and rail traffic is shifted to the alternate approach. When the ship passes the lock and lies between the two approaches, the lock is closed and the water level raised. Meanwhile, the first lift is lowered and trains are rerouted to the original approach, while the newer lift rises to let the ship pass upriver.

Unlike the Lachine Canal, the Montreal-Lachine section of the St. Lawrence Seaway does not cut deep inland, away from the river. Instead, it was constructed by digging a uniform, 27-foot-deep channel directly alongside the south shore of the St. Lawrence. This channel begins just downriver from the Jacques Cartier Bridge, bypasses the river's shallows and rapids, and ends near Lake St. Louis, about a mile upriver from the Honore Mercier Bridge. It is separated from the river by a narrow embankment which expands, just opposite the town of Lasalle and the wildest part of the rapids, to form the grounds of Cote St. Catherine Park.

PUBLIC TRANSIT: Cote St. Catherine Park is, unfortunately, not served by buses. It is possible to connect at the Longueuil Metro station with a bus to La Prairie, but that community is approximately 4 miles distant from the park. The visitor choosing this route would thus have to consider spending more time in transit, on foot, than at his destination.

AUTOMOBILE: Leave Montreal via the Champlain Bridge, and follow the signs for Route 15/132. At La Prairie (about 3 miles from the bridge), bear right onto the turnoff for Boulevard Marie-Victorin East. Follow Marie-Victorin for approximately 4 miles, and turn right at the park sign.

COUNTRY WALKS

Cote St. Catherine is a provincial park, fully equipped for camping. There is both a pool and a lagoon for swimming (campers only), and the entire length of the park's St. Lawrence River shore is popular with trout fishermen. Rainbow and brown trout are stocked annually. The park is located within the Ile aux Herons bird sanctuary. Ile aux Herons itself is visible, along with the smaller Ile au Diable, approximately halfway between the park and the Lasalle shore. If you stand on the river bank near the swimming lagoon and look across, between the two islands, the view will encompass the same vantage points described in Chapter 14 of this book.

THE WALK: The camping season at Cote St. Catherine Park extends between April and September; during the remainder of the year, the park's roads are closed to auto traffic beyond the parking area. Early spring and late fall, then, are a bit quieter here and might be preferred by the day visitor. The most scenic walk within the park is along the river bank. The path extends for about 1¼ miles to the narrow park's western boundary; along the way, keep an eye out for the graceful birds that give the Ile aux Herons sanctuary its name.

Cote St. Catherine Park abuts at its western end the historic Caughnawaga Indian Reserve. This location was originally chosen by Jesuit missionaries, who in 1667 congregated Mohawk and Iroquois converts here to keep them from pagan influences. Later, as the community grew, many Indians came to Caughnawaga on their own. Here was the home of the saintly Kateri Tekakwitha, whose canonization is still being pressed within the Roman Catholic Church; her tomb is nearby on the road from La Prairie to Caughnawaga. The settlement's Indian population was courted over the years by both the French and British. In 1704, during the French ascendancy, Caughnawaga braves were recruited to participate in the bloody assault on Deerfield, Massachusetts. Prisoners taken during the raid were brought back to Caughnawaga, and several of them remained

COTE ST. CATHERINE PARK

there, intermarrying with the Indians. As recently as the 1930's, more than 100 of the descendants of one American captive were still living in the area.

Much later, Caughnawagans served the British in a vastly different capacity. They were the expert canoeists who paddled the Nile during the relief of the beleaguered garrison at Khartoum, in the Sudan. Subjugated themselves, it was the fate of these Iroquois and Mohawks to fight in the colonial wars of their conquerors.

Having walked the length of the park and back along the river, head back towards the entrance and look for the signs indicating the beginning of the bicycle path which leads to Nun's Island and the Victoria Bridge. Although few walkers choose to tackle the entire 8-mile-plus length of the bike path, a walk of only ¼ mile will bring you to the Seaway's St. Catherine Lock.

When a ship travels the length of the St. Lawrence Seaway, it accomplishes a journey not only of 2,000 miles but of 600 vertical feet, the distance in elevation between the Gulf of St. Lawrence and Lake Erie. A system of locks is required to lift and lower Seaway traffic as it ascends or descends the river; at St. Catherine, the variation in water level between the opening and closing of the lock is 36½ feet. The idea behind locks is simple, but the engineering skill represented by a structure such as this is profound, and it is always fascinating to watch an ocean-going behemoth lifted gently along its way to Cleveland, Detroit, or Chicago.

Cyclists can get the best view of the Seaway, and of the river, its bridges, and the city, thanks to an extensive bike path system maintained by Parks Canada. The western end of the path is at Cote St. Catherine Park. From there, it extends along the narrow embankment which separates the Seaway from the river, affording a sensation akin to cycling and boating at the same time. There is no one out there but you, the freighters, and the gulls. The path ends at the Victoria Bridge and the St. Lambert Lock;

here, it would be nice to report that cyclists (or the occasional hardy foot traveler) could find access to Ile Notre Dame, site of the Floralies exhibition (see Chapter 8) and gateway to Ile Ste. Helene, Man and His World, and the Metro. But, as of this writing, this isn't so — return must be via Riverside Drive or a retracking of the Seaway route, or, if you have no car waiting at Cote St. Catherine Park, via Riverside Drive and the Jacques Cartier Bridge to Montreal.

There is an alternate route — just before the Seaway bike path reaches the Champlain Bridge, you will notice a separate, smaller causeway leading across the St. Lawrence to Nun's Island, site of a newly-developed townhouse and apartment community. This bridge is limited to bicycle and pedestrian traffic. It is part of a projected bike route which will eventually lead across Nun's Island and into Montreal; however, as of this writing (summer 1981), cyclists will have to make some provision to return by car from Nun's Island, and pedestrians must rely on the Number 12 bus, which runs from the island to within a few blocks of Lasalle station on Metro Line 1. Using the latter connections, an interesting day trip can be made of a round-trip walk from Nun's Island to the St. Lambert Lock (approximately 6½ miles total).

Cote St. Catherine Provincial Park is open daily between April 1 and November 30; camping is permitted from early June to Labor Day. The park is open between 9 A.M. and 5 P.M. during the non-camping season. For information, call 514-873-2763, 514-873-2843, or 514-632-1510.

The St. Lawrence Seaway Bicycle Path is open between mid-May and mid-October; during the first and last months of the season, access is limited to Saturdays, Sundays, and holidays. Hours vary with the season. For information, call Parks Canada at 514-932-8321 or 514-658-0681.

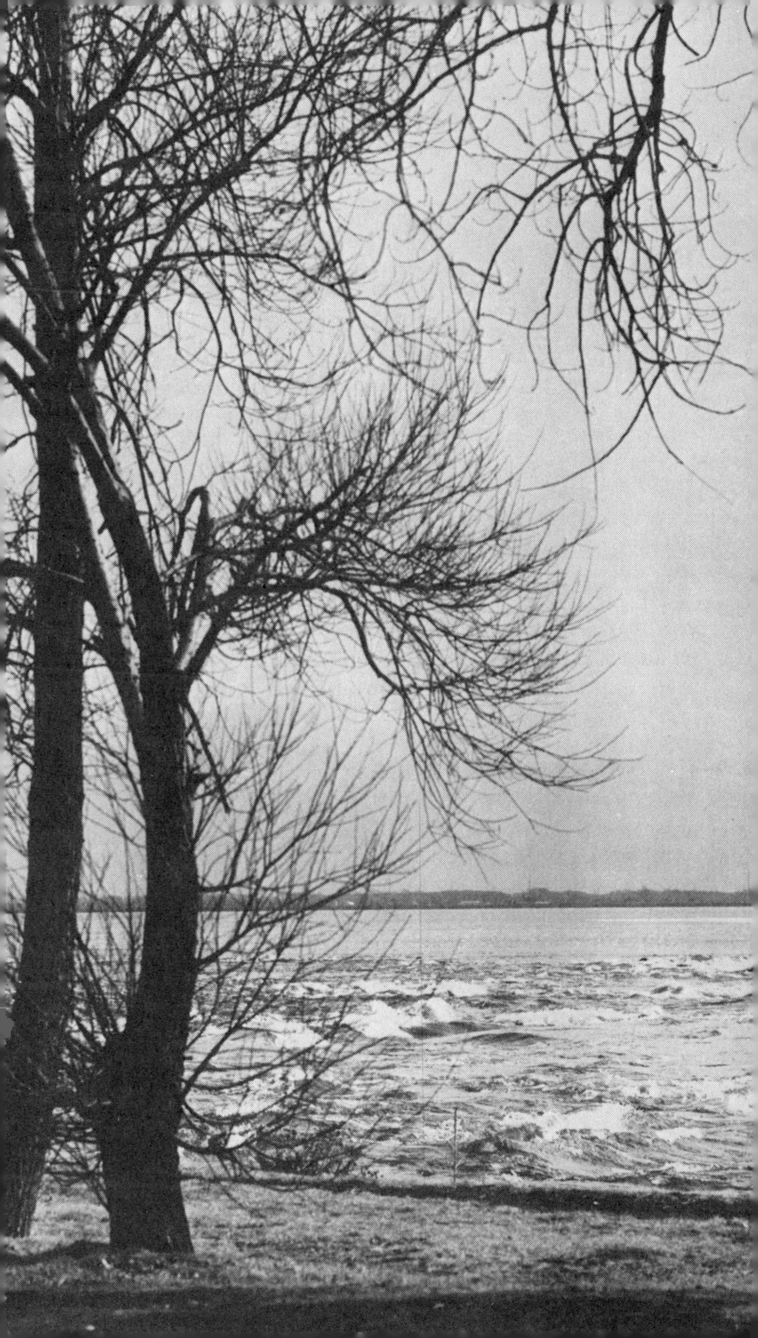

12

RIGAUD

Walking and ski touring, with a 1½-mile trail linking the Shrine of Our Lady of Lourdes, the geologically fascinating "Devil's Garden," and the summit of Rigaud Mountain.

THE STONES STRIKE EACH OTHER with a dull clatter as you walk. It is a curiously hollow sound, and it makes you wonder just how far down the stones go. Here, the earth doesn't seem quite so solid: is this how an insect feels, walking upon grains of sand?

You are crossing a field made entirely of rocks. Not a rocky field, but a field of rocks — no soil, no grass, no trees. It is like a tilting tray of giant irregular marbles, or an inventory of stones with which to stock the rest of Quebec. And where metaphor fails, the legends of the country people — the *habitants* of old Rigaud — take over.

According to the stories, there was a farmer named Baptiste, and he tilled a plot on the north slope of Rigaud Mountain. To help make ends meet, he also went to work cutting timber each spring. One year his plowing took longer than usual, and he began to worry that it would not be done in time for him to leave for logging camp. There seemed to be no solution other than to finish the plowing on a Sunday.

In Baptiste's day, though, the breaking of the Sabbath was a serious matter. So, on Saturday, he went to his parish priest to ask for guidance: should he get the plowing done and his field planted, even though it meant toiling on a Sunday? Or, should

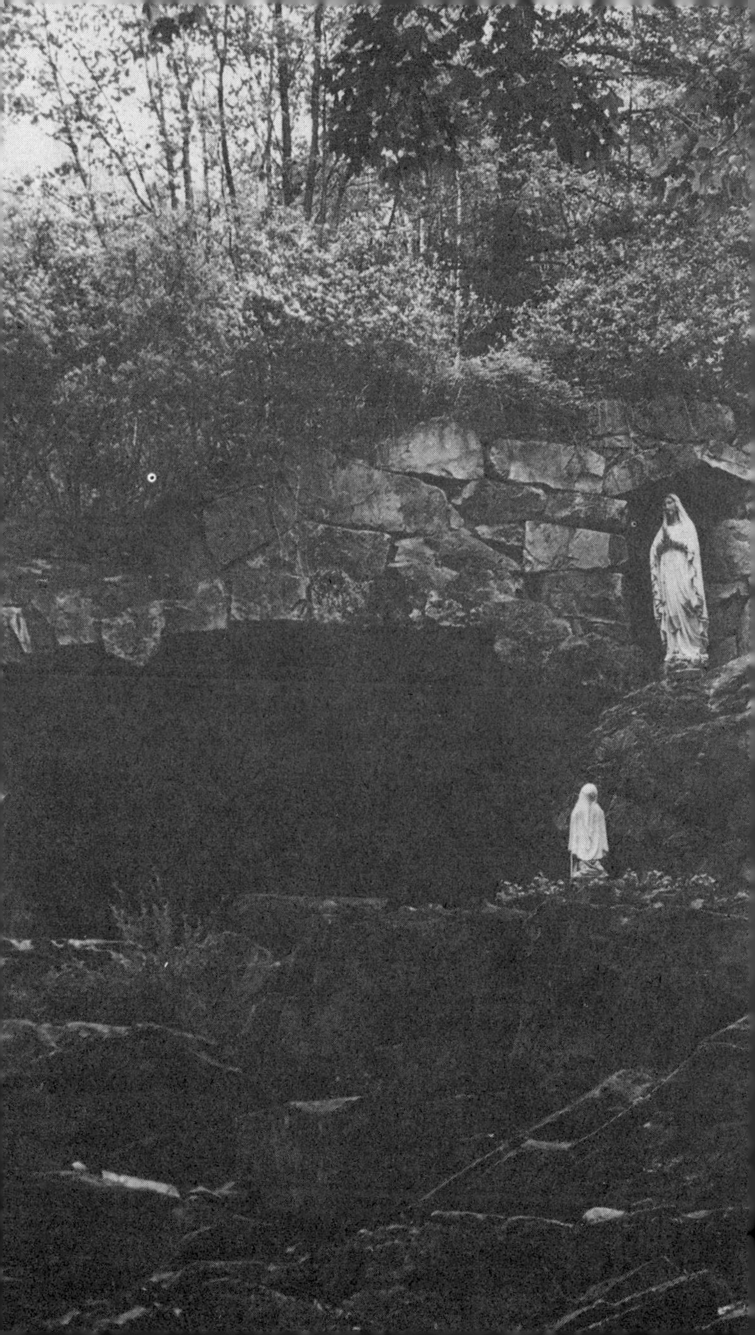

he keep the commandment, and lose a day's earnings in the woods? The priest understood his plight, but found no room for compromise: Baptiste would have to keep his day of rest; to do otherwise would be a mortal sin.

As Baptiste headed home, his dismay turned to defiance. Didn't his family come first? Didn't they need every penny he could make? He resolved to plow until he was finished, and the Devil take the Sabbath.

But, folktales are not known for gentleness of resolution, and the Devil, as it turned out, took Baptiste. He went out to plow on Sunday morning, and that was the last he was heard from. A neighbor stopped by in the afternoon and saw that Baptiste's entire field had turned to stone. There are two versions of what happened to the farmer himself — in one, he too was petrified, along with his horse and plow. In another, he simply sank beneath the stones, taking the short and rocky road to perdition. Thus the name of this formation: the Devil's Garden.

Well, whether or not you believe the story, there is still a field of rocks on Rigaud Mountain. And, the theory offered by geologists to explain its presence is, ironically, one which the old-time *habitants* would have a little trouble swallowing. It involves thousands of years, enormous sheets of ice, and a Rigaud Mountain surrounded by a vast, swollen Lake Champlain.

Rigaud Mountain stands at the western extreme of the Rigaud-Sheffield chain, to which the eight Monteregian hills (see Chapter 3) also belong. Along with St. Andrew's and Oka mountains, it is an outlying projection of the Canadian shield that has been largely stripped of its Paleozoic cover to reveal the Precambrian material of which it is made. In its youth, it was much loftier; today, it rises to a height of about 700 feet above sea level, or 500 feet above the surrounding plain.

Ten thousand years ago, the Wisconsin glacier lumbered across the top of Rigaud Mountain, breaking loose tons of debris. As the ice withdrew, the fragments left on the slopes of the mountain were tumbled and made smooth by a constant flow of meltwater, which also served to wash away sediment and particles of glacial till. The result was the field of mixed

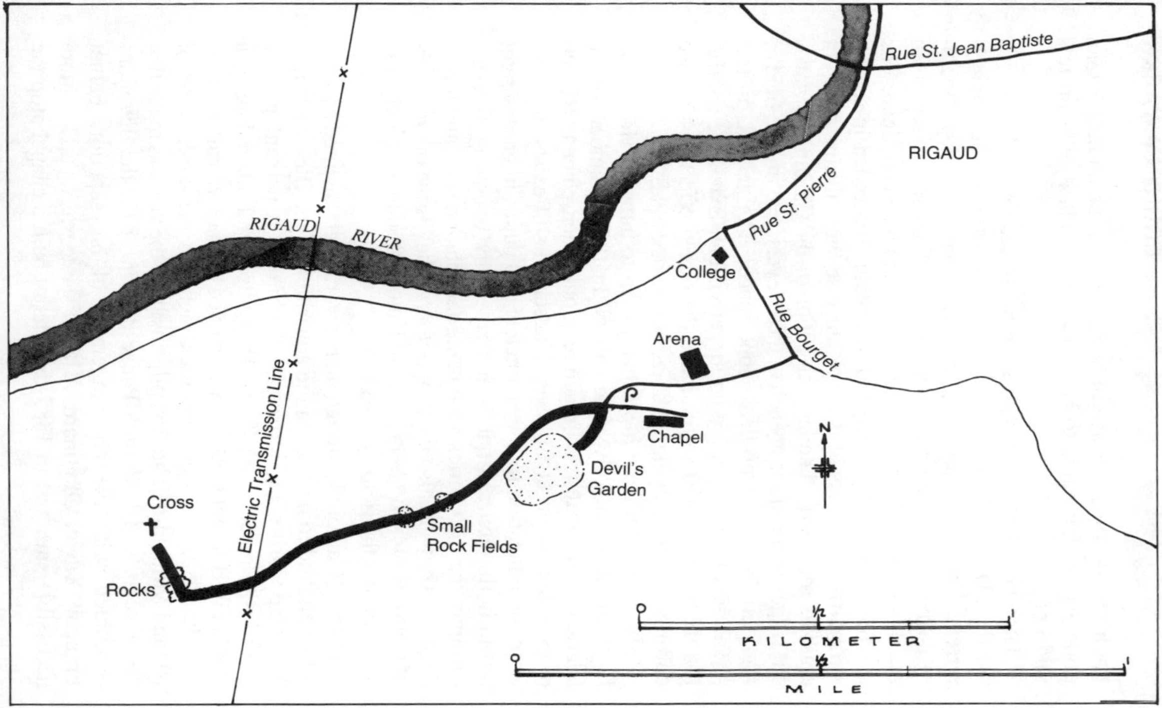
Rue St. Jean Baptiste
RIGAUD
Rue St. Pierre
College
Rue Bourget
RIGAUD
RIVER
Arena
Chapel
Devil's Garden
Electric Transmission Line
Cross
Small Rock Fields
Rocks
N
0
½
1
KILOMETER
0
½
1
MILE

boulders — some the size of basketballs, some no bigger than potatoes — that came to be known as the place of Baptiste's undoing.

There was yet another phase in the formation of the Devil's Garden. During the first few millenia that followed the glacier's retreat, Lake Champlain was far larger than it is today. Geologists have determined its prehistoric outlines, and have given the name "Champlain Sea" to the waters they contained. The sea made an island of Rigaud Mountain. It receded in stages, with different levels of the rock slope serving, during different eras, as the shore. The lapping action of the Champlain waves cut ridges in the slope at each of these levels, leaving the field of boulders with a step-back appearance. The results of this phenomenon, though, are no longer visible. Extensive quarrying during the 1930's eliminated the ridged effect, while also cutting significantly into the size of the rock field.

The Devil does not have this garden to himself. He has, in fact, the most unlikely of neighbors. In 1850, members of the Clerics of St. Viator, a French religious order, came to Rigaud to establish Bourget College. The school still exists, offering Catholic education to approximately 120 pupils in grades eight through thirteen. But it is not solely by operating Bourget College that the Clerics have made a reputation at — and for — Rigaud. They are also the proprietors of the Shrine of Our Lady of Lourdes, which has been carved into the mountain barely 200 yards below the field of stones.

Roman Catholics throughout the world were inspired by what was believed to have been the apparition of the Blessed Virgin Mary appearing to Bernadette Soubirous, a peasant girl, at Lourdes, France in 1858. In 1874, Brother Ludger Pauze, a teacher at Bourget College, was moved to place a small statue of Our Lady of Lourdes in a rock niche on the north slope of Rigaud Mountain. The first pilgrimage to the site was made that same year, and, although Pauze died in 1875, the devotions continued with the encouragement of his superior, Father Francois Xavier Chouinard. A larger statue was set up at a more accessible site, and in 1887 the Clerics built a chapel atop the

RIGAUD

slope. This building survives; it is a small, eight-sided belvedere located just above the grotto where the statue stands.

In 1954, a new chapel was built. This is the open-fronted stone building that stands at the top of the winding road leading up from the college, and at which masses are still offered daily in summer for indoor and outdoor attendants. Here also are a visitor center, gift shop, and restaurant.

A path from the shrine leads to the Devil's Garden, which today appears as a gently sloping, football field-sized area hemmed round by normal, forest-supporting ground. Behind the shrine and "garden" stands the bulk of Rigaud Mountain, most of which is undeveloped. Except for the route leading to the cross (described below), most of the mountain's trails are not well-marked. Hikers wishing to explore the back reaches of the mountain are advised to obtain a topographical map.

PUBLIC TRANSIT: Buses from Montreal to Rigaud are operated by Voyageurs. They depart from the Voyageurs terminal at 505 Maisonneuve East, Montreal. The terminal is located at the Berri de Montigny station, which is accessible via lines 1, 2, and 4. In Rigaud, Voyageurs buses stop at Bourget College on St. Pierre Street. From the college, walk uphill on Bourget Street and follow the signs to the shrine.

AUTOMOBILE: From Montreal, head west on Route 40, the Trans Canada Highway. Take the Rigaud exit and follow Route 342 into town. Turn left onto St. Pierre Street, and left again onto Bourget Street at the college. Follow signs to the shrine.

During the winter, the shrine and its parking lot are closed, and the entrance road is unplowed. The mountain is popular with cross-country skiers, though, and it is permissible to park next to the college arena, just off Bourget Street, and walk or ski up the entrance road to the shrine and its trails.

Rigaud is a small town, located at the point where the Rigaud

COUNTRY WALKS

River empties into the broad Ottawa just east of the Quebec-Ontario border. Its site was part of the seigneury granted in 1732 to Pierre and Francois Rigaud, sons of the Marquis de Vaudreuil. The town's first settlers arrived in 1783. Among them, perhaps, was the unfortunate Baptiste.

THE WALK: The paved pathway to the Devil's Garden begins just to the right of the new chapel. It leads to the rear of this structure and then uphill, past a side trail on the left which ends at the original chapel. After visiting the "Garden," head back to the paved area just left of the new chapel (note: you are now facing downhill, with the chapel at your right), where the 1-mile trail to the summit and cross begins. The trail leads off to the left, just above the rest rooms, and follows a streambed uphill.

Continue past a short cutoff trail, left, that leads to the Devil's Garden; after another several hundred yards you will cross the first of two smaller, isolated rock fields. The trail picks up again directly opposite the entrances to both fields.

About ¼ mile past the last of the two smaller rock fields, the trail enters a glade, to the right of which stands a rising jumble of rock protrusions that can easily be scrambled. This is where a walker will begin to wish that the all-too-infrequent red blazes that mark the trail were a bit clearer. Keep a sharp eye out for red arrows painted on the rocks, but if you don't see any, remember that once you reach the glade, the idea is to turn right, scramble up the rocks, and continue towards higher ground while veering generally towards the left. When the trees are not in leaf, you may be able to use the cross itself as a reference point. The path eventually materializes, and leads up a final, gentle slope directly towards the cross.

The Rigaud summit cross is a simple iron structure erected in 1917. Earlier crosses on this site date to 1844. From the summit,

RIGAUD

you can look down upon the Rigaud River (immediate foreground) and the town (right), and ahead towards Rigaud Bay and the Ottawa. But if your interest runs to wildflowers, be sure to look right in front of you. Rigaud Mountain is home to many unusual varieties, some of which are found nowhere else in Quebec.

The Shrine of Our Lady of Lourdes, Rigaud, Quebec, is open from May 1 to October 31. Between late June and early September, a sound and light show on the apparition at Lourdes is presented at twilight on Tuesdays, Thursdays, Saturdays, and Sundays. For information, call 514-451-0390/4631.

13

ILES DE BOUCHERVILLE PROVINCIAL PARK

Walking and bicycling — 4½ miles of foot and bike trails on Ile Ste. Marguerite, with footbridges and further trail development planned for four other islands. A provincial park surrounded by water, just north of downtown Montreal, the Iles de Boucherville have remained largely obscure since their days as part of a land grant to one of the old seigneurs of New France.

BICYCLING ALONG A GRAVEL PATH on Ile Ste. Marguerite, you flush a brace of grouse and watch their steep, fast ascent above the stone's-throw-breadth stream — improbably named "Chenal Grand Riviere" — that separates you from Ile St. Jean. The birds do not cross the water; they arc back and drop into the brambles of a little cover. But, you continue looking to the west-northwest, beyond the fields and bracken of Ile St. Jean, Ile a Pinard, and Ile Tourte Blanche. Far across the main channel of the St. Lawrence, on the Island of Montreal, bristle the stacks of the Shell refinery, which inhales crude that has been tankered down the thousand miles from the sea.

The terrain of these islands is smooth; you can also easily see the parish spires of Boucherville and Longueuil on the nearer, opposite shore. The city lies upstream; ahead, the swift St. Lawrence rushes to its confluence — at Trois Rivieres — with the Riviere des Prairies and Riviere des Mille Iles.

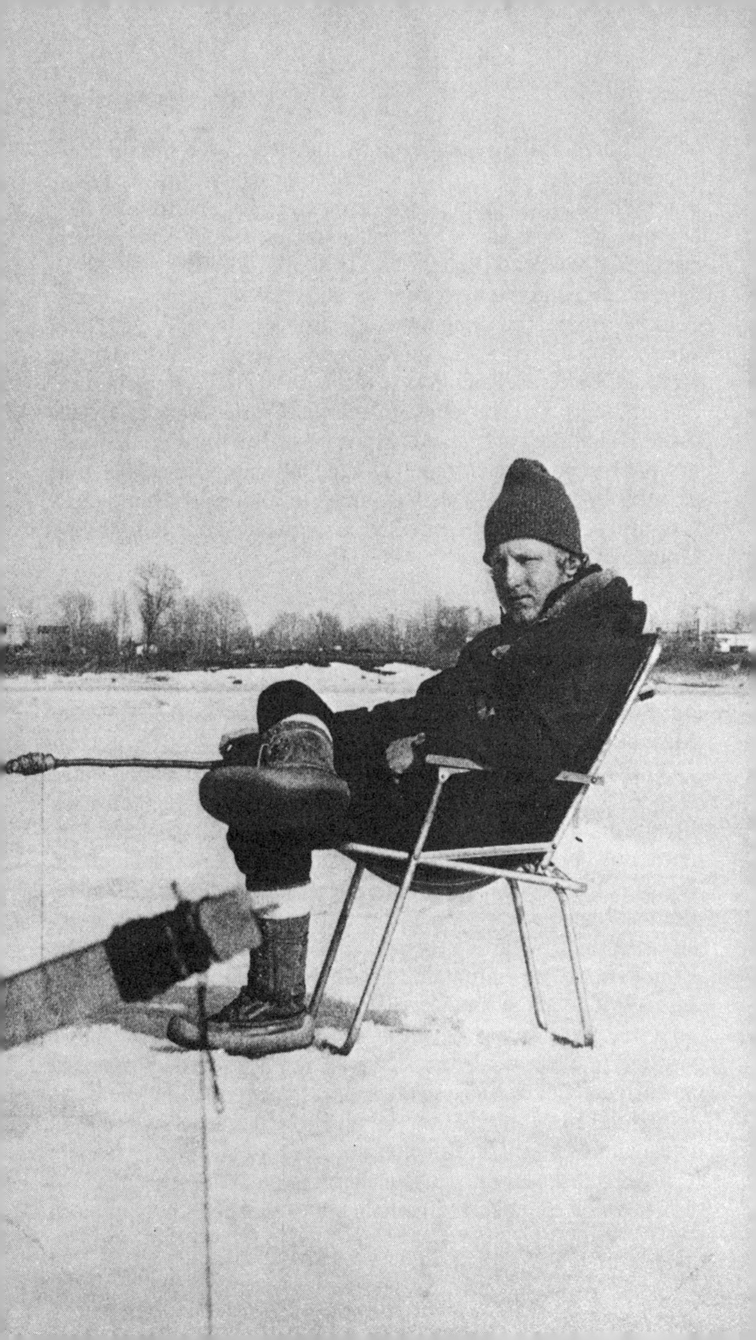

COUNTRY WALKS

Anchored amidstream in the St. Lawrence, the Iles de Boucherville comprise Quebec's newest provincial park. Taken together, the little archipelago made up of Ile Charron, Ile Ste. Marguerite (these two are now actually one island, having been connected by landfill), Ile St. Jean, Ile a Pinard, Ile de la Commune, and Ile Grosbois extends for 4½ miles and encompasses an area three times as large as Mount Royal Park. There is, in fact, even more to this cluster of islands: the Grandes Battures Tailhandier, made up of Ile La Fontaine, Ile Dufaut, and the abovementioned Ile Tourte Blanche (white turtle) flank the park islands to the west. But these are federal, not provincial, property, and as such are slated for designation as a bird sanctuary. This will bring to a close the hunting of migratory waterfowl, which still attracts sportsmen to the Grandes Battures.

As of this writing, trails and picnic areas have been developed only on Ile Ste. Marguerite. But, by the summer of 1982 or 1983, bridges between each of the major islands will be completed, and it will be possible to make a circuit of the entire park on foot. Automobiles, though, will be confined to Ile Ste. Marguerite.

These quiet, grassy islands — only Grosbois, as the name suggests, is heavily forested, although the park's planners have invested a half million dollars in new tree plantings — have up until now been one of the least known and least appreciated features of the local geography. More than a few Montrealers draw a blank when they are mentioned, and we might easily surmise that this group includes daily commuters who use the Louis-Hippolyte-Lafontaine Tunnel, which metamorphoses into a bridge at the southern tip of Ile Charron.

But, by no means have the Iles Boucherville spent history waiting to become a provincial park. Their story begins almost as early as that of Maisonneuve's settlement of Ville Marie, on the island of Montreal, and involves another of New France's great names — Pierre Boucher.

Twelve-year-old Pierre Boucher arrived in French Canada in 1634, when Samuel de Champlain was still governor. In those

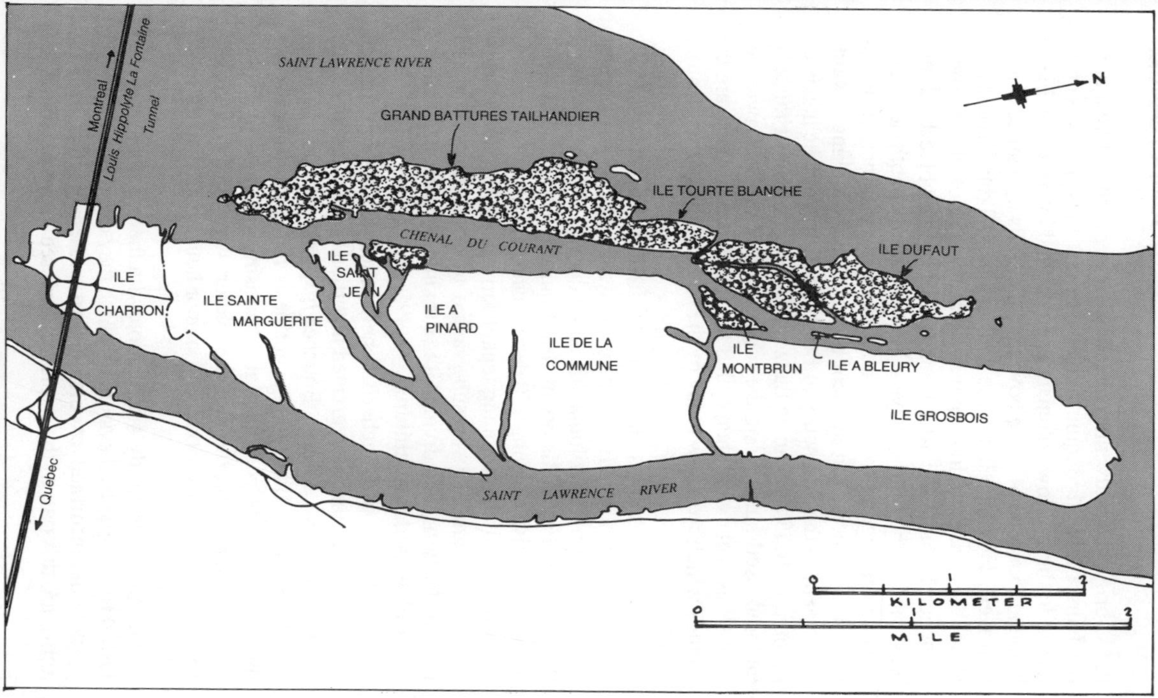
SAINT LAWRENCE RIVER
N
Montreal
Louis Hippolyte La Fontaine
Tunnel
GRAND BATTURES TAILHANDIER
ILE TOURTE BLANCHE
CHENAL DU COURANT
ILE DUFAUT
ILE
CHARRON
ILE SAINTE
MARGUERITE
ILE
SAINT
JEAN
ILE A
PINARD
ILE DE LA
COMMUNE
ILE
MONTBRUN
ILE A BLEURY
ILE GROSBOIS
SAINT LAWRENCE RIVER
Quebec
0
1
2
KILOMETER
0
1
2
MILE

days, bright and adventurous lads were sent out to live among the Huron and Algonquin Indians, so that they might become useful to their fellow colonists as guides and interpreters. Pierre Boucher was one of those boys, and the skills he learned served him well. He made his name and fortune at Trois Rivieres, of which he was appointed governor at the age of 30. In 1661, Boucher became the first Canadian to be ennobled by Louis XIV, and in the following year he successfully petitioned Louis to send the regular troops to help the settlers in their struggles with the Iroquois. But by then, he was already looking towards retirement to the Seigneury of Boucherville, which he had been granted in 1655 by Jean de Lauzon, governor of New France. It encompassed lands along the south shore of the St. Lawrence, as well as what were then called the Iles Percees. These are the islands which we know today by the name of the old seigneurial grant.

Boucher held to his plans, and "retired" to his lands in 1667, when he was forty-five. There he wrote one of the earliest secular accounts of colonial life along the St. Lawrence, entitled "A True and Frank History of New France." There also he lived to be ninety-five, leaving 150 descendants. Like other seigneurs, he parceled his land among tenant farmers — Ile Ste. Marguerite, for example, was sub-granted to Louis Lamoreux and Francis Boivin, who divided it in turn into six parts held among themselves and their children.

Another one of Boucher's beneficiaries was his son, Ignace Boucher, to whom was granted a portion of Ile Grosbois, then known as Ile St. Joseph. Boucher *fils,* who took the surname "de Grosbois," died young, but he is remembered partly for having served as godfather at a baptism performed by Father Jacques Marquette, the famed explorer, who lived and worked for a while at Pierre Boucher's manor house on the south shore of the St. Lawrence.

The Boucher family's affiliation with these islands long outlasted the seigneurial system to which they owed them. A 1906 guidebook informed excursion boat passengers that as they approach this part of the river, they will see "several islands, of

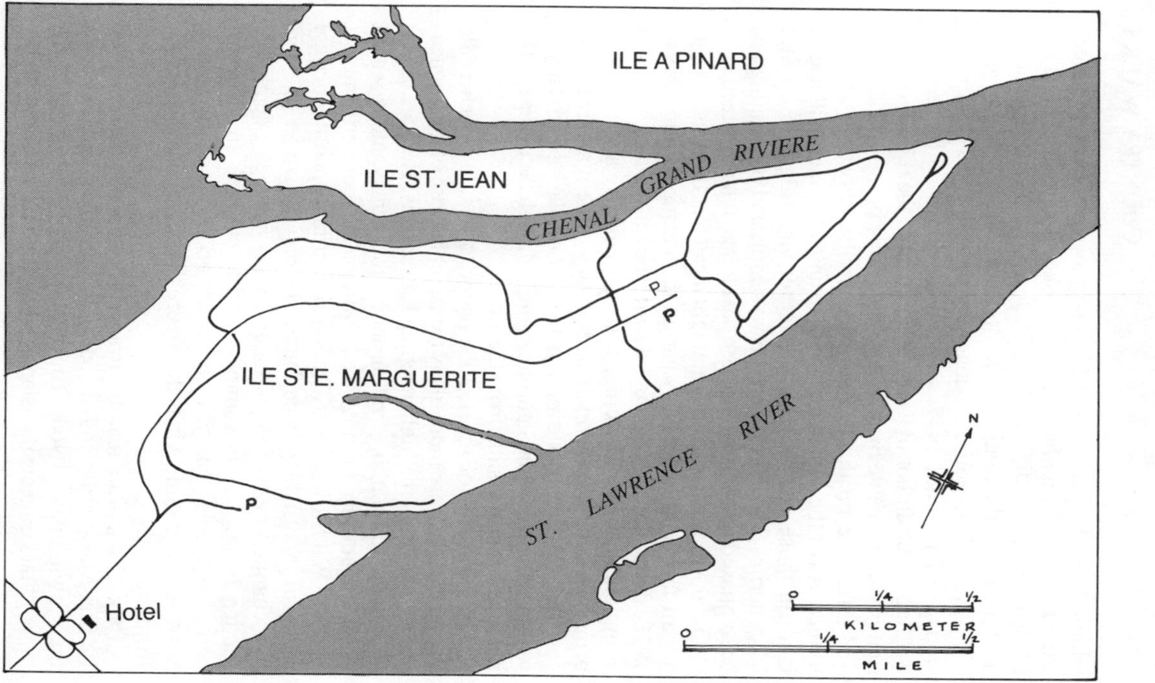
ILE A PINARD
ILE ST. JEAN
CHENAL GRAND RIVIERE
ILE STE. MARGUERITE
ST. LAWRENCE RIVER
P
P
P
Hotel
N
0
1/4
1/2
KILOMETER
0
1/4
1/2
MILE

which the principal, crowned by enormous elm trees, produces from afar the effect of an immense basket of verdure. This is the Ile de Grosbois, called also Isle St. Joseph, and is occupied by a descendant of the family of De Boucherville, who had given it his name." The house inhabited by this unnamed descendant stood, in fact, until 1947, when it was destroyed by fire. According to the author of a recent monograph, the ruined foundation is still traceable in an overgrown corner of this island.

Agriculture on the Iles de Boucherville has survived even longer. As of the summer of 1980, mainland farmers still leased land on those islands which were not yet bridged to Ile Ste. Marguerite. The exclusive crop was corn, and its planting has been phased out only as the park development has proceeded.

Older Montrealers, though, might recall that Ile Grosbois was not all farmland in the early part of this century. From 1909 to 1928, it was the site of King Edward Park, an amusement resort complete with horse racing, a scenic railway, and ferries to bring patrons from the mainland. Today, little remains to suggest that Ile Grosbois ever was the sort of place to which you would bring a date on Saturday night, although the outline of the racetrack is still visible from the air.

The pleasures of the 1980's visitor to Iles de Boucherville Provincial Park are more likely to resemble those of the seigneurial tenants than the high-stepping Edwardians. Here are extensive paths for walking and meadows for picnics, along with a complete absence of motorized traffic on the four northernmost islands. Wildflower identification and birding opportunities are plentiful, and fishing is permitted. During the winter, the narrow channels between the islands usually freeze to a depth safe for ice fishing; as in summer, catfish and pike are the most common species taken. Don't count on cross-country skiing, however. The same winds that freeze the river scour snow cover from the trails.

Park officials are making arrangements for bicycle rentals on Ile Ste. Marguerite, and of course visitors are welcome to bring their own bikes. (Note: Bicyclists cannot pass through the tunnel that connects the islands with Montreal.) The possibility

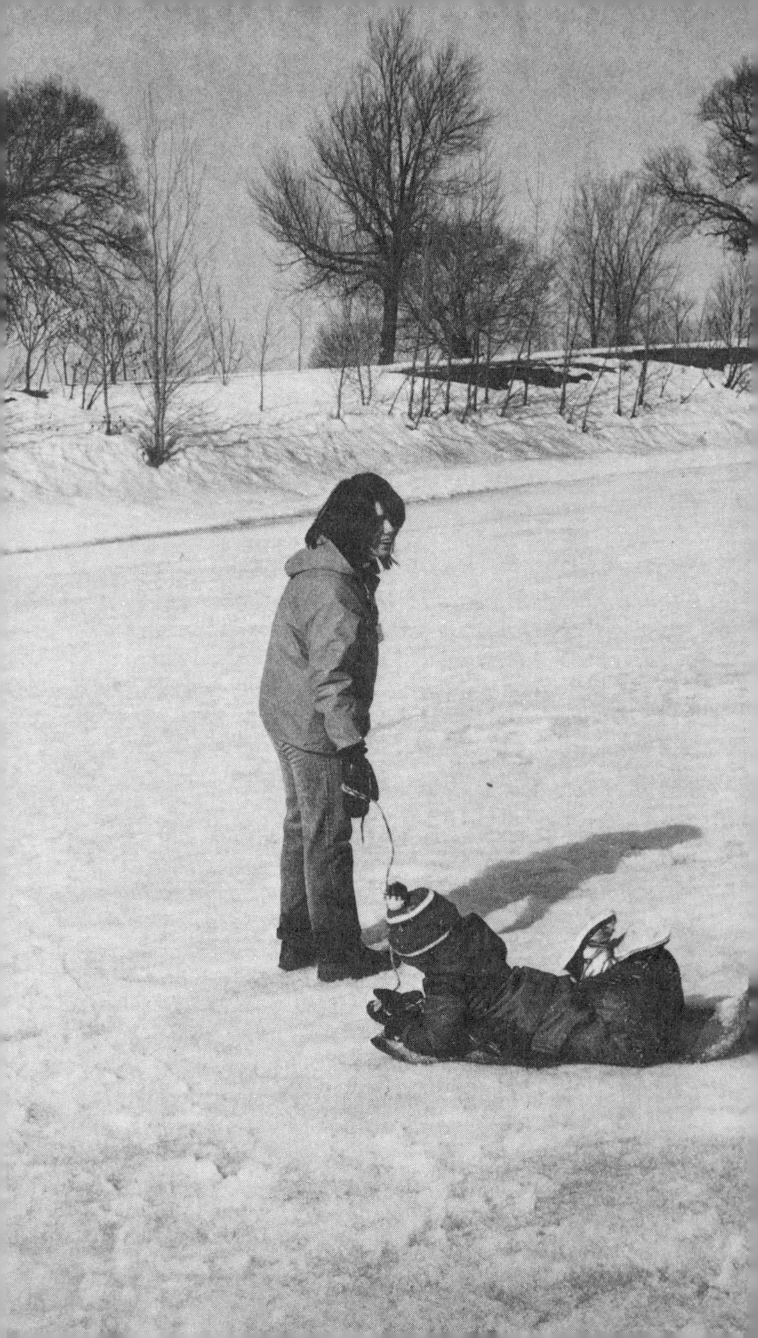

COUNTRY WALKS

of rowboat and canoe rentals is being explored, as is a program of guided nature walks. Camping is not allowed and fires must be confined to portable barbecues.

PUBLIC TRANSIT: From the Radisson Metro station, the next-to-last stop on Metro Line 1, take the No. 61 bus to Ile Charron. Shortly after emerging from the Louis-Hippolyte-La Fontaine Tunnel, the bus will stop at the small Sheraton Hotel on Ile Charron. Get off here; the park entrance is to the left of the hotel. During busier seasons, authorities expect that buses will pick up and discharge passengers within the park, rather than at the gate. A waiting area has been constructed for this purpose.

AUTOMOBILE: From downtown Montreal, take either Sherbrooke or Route 40 (Metropolitan Boulevard), turning east onto Route 25, which leads into the Louis-Hippolyte-La Fontaine Tunnel. Take the Ile Charron exit (first exit after emerging from tunnel), which loops across Route 25 and leads to the Sheraton Hotel, right, and the park entrance, directly ahead. Continue past the entrance to the designated parking area.

THE WALK: Trails on the islands are divided into those open to both cyclists and walkers, and those closed to all except foot travel. One of the accompanying maps shows the system of trails which has been developed on Ile Ste. Marguerite; the other shows the entire chain of islands prior to construction of bicycle and pedestrian bridges. The best trails for waterfowl observation are those which most closely follow the islands' shorelines; keep an eye on marshy areas along the narrower passages and on backwaters and blind channels, such as those which punctuate Ile St. Jean. If you make your way up to Ile Grosbois, you may wish to see if you can find traces of the old racetrack. It's impossible to give pinpoint directions; however, old

ILES DE BOUCHERVILLE PROVINCIAL PARK

maps show the park to have been at the southern end of the island, with the track just north of the southeastern corner.

Iles de Boucherville Provincial Park, Boucherville, Quebec, is open daily from 7 A.M. until sunset. For information, call 514-873-2843.

14

ANGRIGNON PARK — AQUEDUCT CANAL — LACHINE RAPIDS

Walking, ski touring, and bicycling — 7 miles (slightly longer from Metro). A new path follows Montreal's Aqueduct Canal into the town of Lasalle, where it empties into the St. Lawrence just above the Lachine Rapids. Return along the river, with a close-up view of the rapids.

HERE IS A WALK WHICH, like the Lachine Canal route described in Chapter 11, parallels an old urban waterway on the tip of Montreal Island. The two are also similar in that neither is a true "country" excursion; however, both begin and end at Angrignon Park and provide a rare opportunity for ski, bicycle, or foot travel without interference from city traffic. The circuit suggested here offers the extra attraction of walking alongside the thundering Lachine Rapids.

PUBLIC TRANSIT: From downtown Montreal, take Metro Line 1 to Angrignon station. This is the last stop for westbound trains. Enter the park, and follow the main road past the swimming and skating areas. The road curves to the left around the tip of the park's lake, and leads to the parking lot at the de la Verendrye Boulevard gate. In winter, you can ski this route.

St. Lawrence River, near the outlet of the Aqueduct Canal

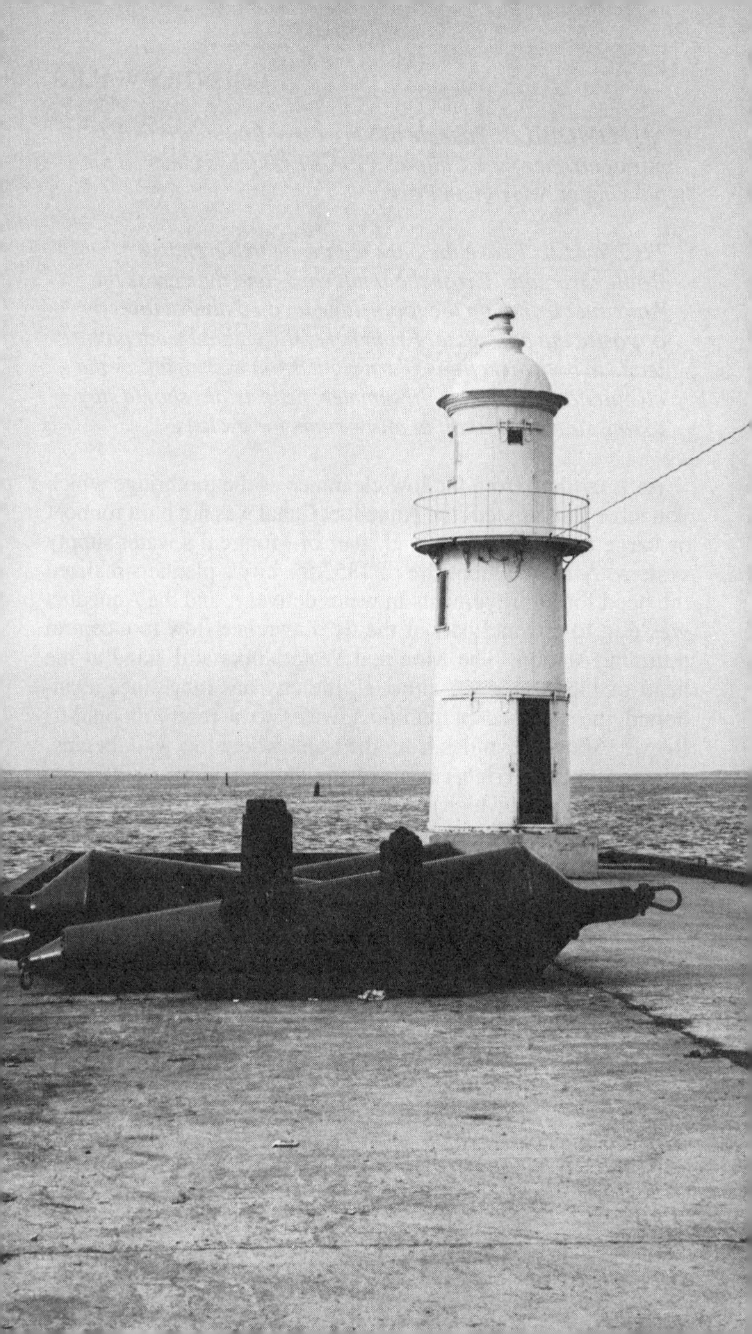

COUNTRY WALKS

AUTOMOBILE: Take de la Verendrye Boulevard to the park entrance (see Chapter 7). A $1.00 fee is charged for parking at Angrignon Park.

THE WALK: Leave the park via the de la Verendrye Boulevard gate. Cross the boulevard, and then cross the Aqueduct Canal on the footbridge located almost directly opposite the park gate. From here, the embankment path leads in both directions. Turn right if you wish to follow the circuit described here. In summer, pedestrians should stay to one side of the path to allow room for cyclists.

As is evident from the low clearance of the footbridge which you have just crossed, the Aqueduct Canal was not built for boat or barge traffic. It is, instead, part of Montreal's water supply system. After the great fire of 1852 the city's planners realized the need for improvements in water delivery, and the Aqueduct was dug to channel part of the St. Lawrence flow to a central pumping station. The Montreal Waterworks still stand at the head of the Aqueduct, although the city has long since abandoned the practice of pumping water to a reservoir on Mt. Royal. About 1½ miles from the point where this walk begins, on the opposite (right) bank of the Aqueduct, you will see a purification plant which is part of the present-day water system.

Continue along the Aqueduct Canal until you reach Quenneville Bay, in the city of Lasalle, where the manmade waterway meets the St. Lawrence. If you have been traveling on skis, you can simply reverse direction and return to Angrignon Park — or, you can turn right onto Lasalle Boulevard, cross the bridge, walk along the river for 2 miles, and return to the park via a reverse of the Lachine Canal route described in Chapter 11. The Number 109 bus also links the Aqueduct and Lachine canals. (Distance from Angrignon Park to end of Aqueduct Canal approximately 2½ miles.)

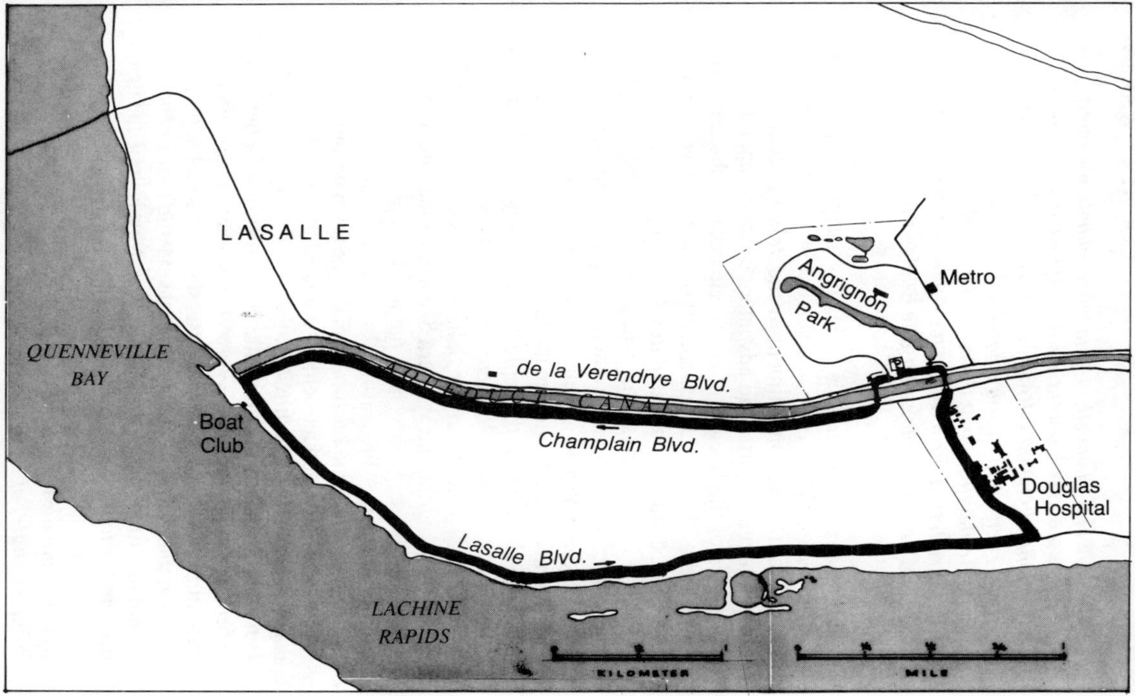
LASALLE
Metro
Angrignon Park
QUENNEVILLE BAY
de la Verendrye Blvd.
AQUEDUCT CANAL
Boat Club
Champlain Blvd.
Douglas Hospital
Lasalle Blvd.
LACHINE RAPIDS
KILOMETER
MILE

COUNTRY WALKS

For walkers and cyclists, and those who do not mind carrying their skis, the return route along the St. Lawrence is recommended. And, if snow cover is adequate, skiers need not even unbind, since parkland parallels much of Lasalle Boulevard along the river. To begin the return route, turn left at the outlet of the Aqueduct, pass the boat club, and head east along Lasalle Boulevard.

Robert Cavelier, Sieur de la Salle, was the quintessential Kid with Big Ideas. When he was a student in Rouen, France, he eagerly awaited each installment of the *Jesuit Relations*, that seventeenth-century true-life adventure series compiled by the missionaries of the Society of Jesus. He became obsessed with the notion that the French settlements on the St. Lawrence were only a short distance via *Canot du Maitre* from the mysterious East, and it is no surprise that when, at age 23, he traveled to New France to visit his brother, he quickly dismissed any thought of going back to Rouen. Instead, he obtained a seigneury on the Island of Montreal from the landholding Sulpician order, and built his house near the rapids which Samuel de Champlain had named St. Louis. No merchant, priest, or Indian passing this point was safe from La Salle's incessant interrogations regarding passage to the Western Sea and China, and it wasn't long before the seigneury, and the nearby rapids, came to be known as La Chine. Present-day Lachine, though, lies upriver, on the other side of the Lachine Canal. The town we are in now, as we leave the Aqueduct behind and head towards the rapids, was named after La Salle himself.

But, it is the romance of La Salle, and not his tenure here, that is celebrated in the name. By 1669, just three years after his arrival in New France, the ambitious seigneur sold his property and began the exploration and fur-trade machinations which led him, not to China, but to the mouth of the Mississippi and death at the hands of a colonist in his party.

Continue east along Lasalle Boulevard. About a mile from the outlet of the Aqueduct Canal, the rapids start to

ANGRIGNON PARK

grow angrier, and at a point approximately 2½ miles from the Aqueduct you will come upon a causeway leading to a small park, which occupies a narrow island set in an especially turbulent section of the river.

Walk out onto the island. If sight and sound alone are not enough to convince you of the water's fury, take note of the signs which warn fishermen that they must wear lifejackets when approaching the banks. In the spring, when meltwater adds to the speed and volume of the rapids, it is hard to imagine a lifejacket doing much good for anyone unlucky enough to fall in.

Today, we can stand alongside the Lachine Rapids and admire their sheer, restless power. But, to the early settlers and explorers, the rapids were less a matter of beauty and excitement than of simple frustration. For a thousand miles, New France's river highway flowed unimpeded, offering seagoing vessels access from the banks of Newfoundland to the very heart of the continent. And then, suddenly, the St. Lawrence erupted over rock-strewn shallows that could slice the bottom from a ship. The portage at Lachine became the first famous overland carry in a nation whose commerce depended on its lakes, rivers, and streams. The fur trail stretched 4,000 miles from Montreal to Astoria, on Oregon's Pacific Coast, and all but 5 percent of that distance could be covered in a canoe. The Lachine Rapids served to warn the *coureurs du bois* and *voyageurs* of those stubborn miles which remained to be traveled on foot.

But, as impractical as it may have been to regularly run the rapids in freight-laden commercial craft, a skillful pilot could bring a nimble vessel through in one piece. Samuel de Champlain is recorded as the first white man to have safely made the trip; he was guided through by Indians in June of 1611. In 1843, someone got up the nerve to send a steamship into the torrent. That ship was the *Ontario*, and her story has as much to do with cleverness as with bravado.

The *Ontario* was built at Niagara in 1840, but her buyers wished to use her for the Montreal-Quebec mail run. In those days, no ship her size had ever been sailed on the St. Lawrence below Prescott, Ontario. How would she be delivered?

COUNTRY WALKS

The *Ontario's* owners turned to two Indian pilots, who were regarded as the best on the river, and offered them each $1,000 if they could get her safely past the rapids. The pilots responded to the challenge by ordering the construction of a dummy boat of pine floats from which 10-foot-long stakes protruded down into the water. This they launched at a point above the rapids, while other Indians waited downstream to observe the makeshift craft's passage. When the dummy boat reached calm water, it was removed and overturned. None of the protruding spikes had been damaged. Thus the pilots knew that there was enough water — in at least one channel — to safely float the new steamer.

Next, the Indians who had watched from shore got aboard the *Ontario*, and each guided it through that portion of the rapids which he had studied during the test run. The experiment was a success — although no steamship followed until 1858. Throughout these early years, Indians were the pilots of choice on the Lachine Rapids. It is not known, however, whether they shared their earnings with their shoreside observers.

By 1870, there was actually a small excursion boat — the *Beauharnois* — that carried tourists through the rapids. In favorable weather, it made regular runs between Lachine and downtown Montreal. As strange as it may seem, people flocked onto the Lachine trains, in order to return to the city via the exciting new water route.

To complete your less exciting but infinitely safer trip, continue along Lasalle Boulevard until you reach the greenhouse opposite the grounds of the Douglas Hospital. (Length of walk along Lasalle Boulevard, approximately 3½ miles.) Turn left at the main gate and enter the hospital grounds; at this point, in winter, you may put your skis back on. Walk through to the Champlain Boulevard exit at the rear of the hospital grounds, opposite which there is a footbridge across the Aqueduct Canal. Cross de la Verendrye Boulevard, turn left, and return to the Angrignon Park entrance and parking lot. If you wish to return instead

ANGRIGNON PARK

to the Angrignon Metro station, turn right on de la Verendrye Boulevard, then left on Des Trinitaires, which parallels the park and leads to the station. (Note: If your car isn't waiting at Angrignon Park, you can walk two miles farther along the city of Verdun's riverside park, which extends along Lasalle Boulevard past the Douglas Hospital turnoff. Continue as far as Avenue De L'Eglise and turn left. The De L'Eglise Metro stop, on Line 1, is only a block away.)

15

ILE DE LA VISITATION/RIVIERE DES PRAIRIES/BOISE HERITAGE

A trip to the northern and eastern reaches of the island of Montreal, where we find three parks-in-the-making which will considerably expand the horizons of area walkers, ski tourers, and cyclists.

HERE ARE THREE PARKS, all currently under development by the Urban Community of Montreal. The first, Ile de la Visitation, borders upon a residential neighborhood on the northern shore of Montreal Island. The others — Riviere des Prairies and Boise Heritage — are located at the island's eastern extreme, in an area which has retained much of its rural character but which is beginning to feel increasing development pressures. The creation of these parks involves not only the preservation of important green spaces, but an ambitious program of reforestation; bicycle, ski, and foot path construction; and, the reclamation of a scenic and historic riverfront for recreational purposes.

Of the three new parks, Ile de la Visitation is the smallest and the nearest to downtown Montreal. It is also, as of this writing, the closest to completion. Although several of its parking and visitor reception areas have yet to be constructed,ns trail network is essentially intact and is already well patronized.

Ile de la Visitation is an island in name only; it is anchored to Montreal proper by the Papineau-Le Blanc Bridge, and by a

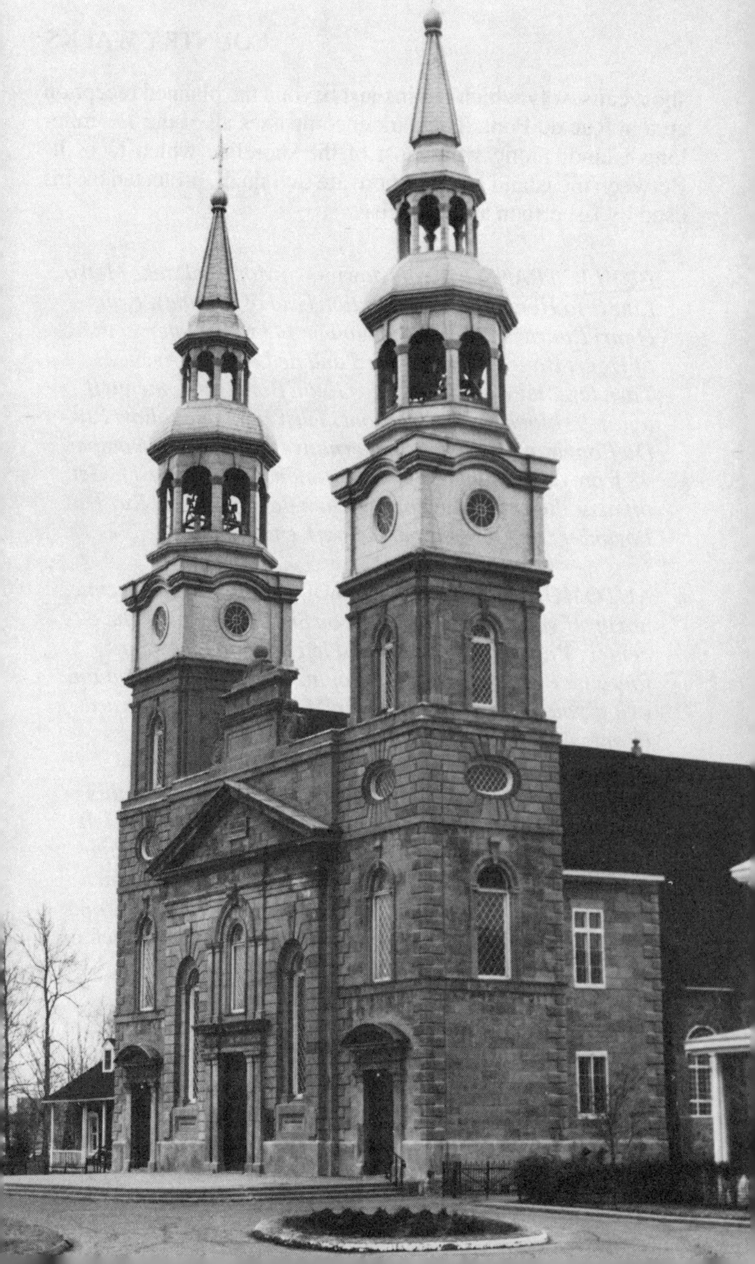

COUNTRY WALKS

short causeway which begins just beyond the planned reception area at Rue du Pont. The park encompasses all of the 1½-mile-long island, along with most of the shoreline which faces it. Between the island and the shore are two small, protected basins used by fishermen and canoeists.

PUBLIC TRANSIT: From downtown Montreal, take Metro Line 2 to Henri Bourassa station (end of the line). From Henri Bourassa, take bus Number 143 to the intersection of Henri Bourassa Boulevard and de Lorimier Avenue. Turn left and walk 1 block to Gouin Boulevard, then left again ½ block to Rue Du Pont. Turn right and follow Rue Du Pont into the park. An alternative is to take bus Number 45 from downtown (Papineau station, Metro Line 1). Get off near the end of the line at Gouin Boulevard and Rue De Lorimier, one block from the park entrance.

AUTOMOBILE: From downtown, take Papineau Avenue north. If you are heading east on Sherbrooke from the city center, Papineau is the second left after you pass Lafontaine Park. Or, take the Papineau Avenue northbound exit if you are traveling east on Metropolitan Boulevard (Route 40). As you approach the Papineau-Le Blanc Bridge, stay to the right. Take the last exit before the bridge, and turn right onto Gouin Boulevard. As of this writing, there is limited parking along Rue Du Pont (left turn from Gouin Boulevard); however, the park's major lots will be located off nearby Rue D'Iberville. To reach these parking areas, turn right from Papineau Avenue onto Henri Bourassa Boulevard, just before Gouin, then left on Rue D'Iberville.

THE WALK: Final plans for Ile de la Visitation call for paved bicycle paths as well as foot trails, along with a footbridge linking the mainland with the island in the vicinity of the dam near its eastern tip. While the bridge is not likely to be completed before 1983, visitors can use the

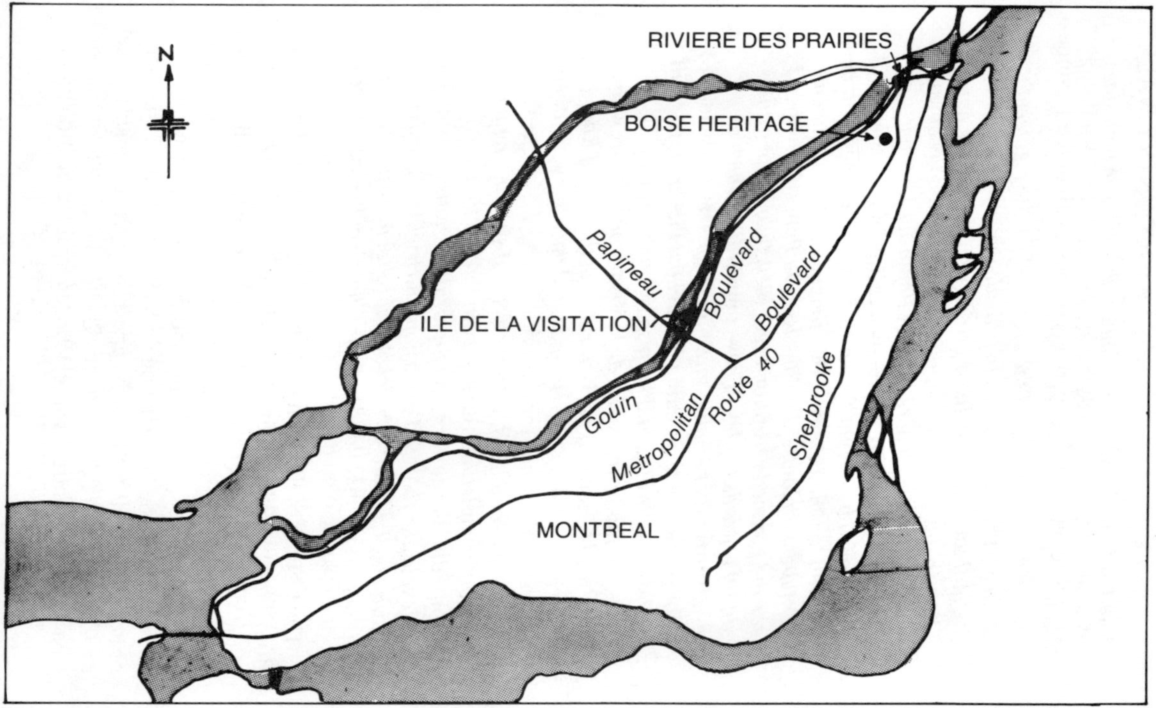
N
RIVIERE DES PRAIRIES
BOISE HERITAGE
Papineau
Boulevard
Boulevard
ILE DE LA VISITATION
40
Route
Gouin
Metropolitan
Sherbrooke
MONTREAL

COUNTRY WALKS

Rue Du Pont causeway to connect the trails on both sides. The island has long been accessible at this point; Rue Du Pont is built along an impoundment constructed by the Sulpician proprietors of the area early in the eighteenth century. Their object was to provide water power for a sawmill and, later, mills to grind grain. Hence the name "Bassin des Moulins," applied to the small body of water which lies between here and the Papineau-Le Blanc Bridge. Of the buildings located in this vicinity, some will be removed by the park's developers, while others will be allowed to remain during the lifetimes of their occupants.

On the mainland side of the Rue Du Pont causeway, near the planned reception area, bicycle and foot trails lead off towards the left. These same trails, which extend for approximately 1 mile, are blazed for skiers in winter. Reforestation is proceeding throughout this area; this will provide windbreaks and keep snow on the trails. The projected footbridge to Ile de la Visitation will link with these trails, as will a park entrance at the foot of Rue D'Iberville. A playing field and small open-air amphitheater are also planned for this area.

On the island itself, a trail circuit of similar length is nearing completion. Access is via Rue Du Pont and, eventually, the eastern-end footbridge. Plans also call for a bicycle and foot trail extension which will pass under the Papineau-Le Blanc Bridge and parallel that structure on its way to the mainland and the Church of the Visitation.

The Church of the Visitation, which is located just off Gouin Boulevard to the left of the Papineau-Le Blanc Bridge approach, is the oldest church on the island of Montreal. The beautifully decorated nave dates to 1749-51, while the twin steeples flanking the entrance were built in 1850. The full French name of the church, Eglise de la Visitation du Sault-au-Recollet, commemorates the Franciscan Recollet priests who accompanied Samuel de Champlain to this site in 1615. On June 24 of that year, the first Mass in Montreal was celebrated by these missionaries on

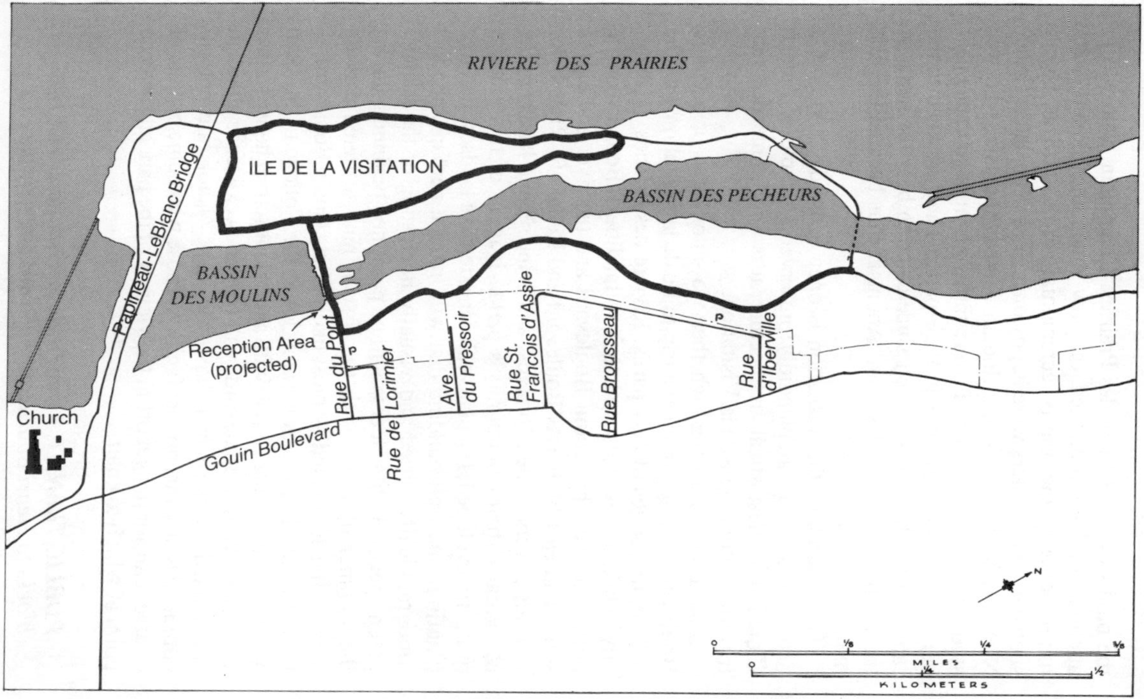

RIVIERE DES PRAIRIES
ILE DE LA VISITATION
BASSIN DES PECHEURS
BASSIN DES MOULINS
Papineau-LeBlanc Bridge
Reception Area (projected)
Church
Gouin Boulevard
Rue du Pont
Rue de Lorimier
Ave. du Pressoir
Rue St. Francois d'Assie
Rue Brousseau
Rue d'Iberville
P
P
N
0
1/8
1/4
3/8
MILES
0
1/4
1/2
KILOMETERS

COUNTRY WALKS

the banks of the Riviere des Prairies. Champlain, who was in attendance, later remarked on how much the Indians were impressed with the priests' ceremonial vestments. But, not all such early encounters were happy ones. Ten years later, Father Nicholas Viel and a young Indian named Ahuntsic, who was studying for the priesthood, were thrown from their canoe near here by traitorous Hurons in their party. They drowned in the rapids (French, *sault*), which since came to bear the name of their religious order. Viel and Ahuntsic thus became the first martyrs in New France.

The Church of the Visitation is open every day. As both a historical site and a splendidly preserved example of French Canadian ecclesiastical architecture, it is a recommended side trip for visitors to Ile de la Visitation.

It is a simple matter, whether via automobile or a Gouin Boulevard bus, to combine a trip to Ile de la Visitation with the next in this series of new parks, Riviere des Prairies. (Eventually, a bikeway will also link the two facilities.) Bounded on the north and west by Gouin Boulevard and the river and on the south and east by Perras Boulevard and Route 40, Riviere des Prairies covers some 386 acres, and is the second largest of the Montreal Urban Community's parks. It is, as of this writing, quite undeveloped, but plans call for extensive landscaping, tree planting, and trail building that will make it perhaps the most topographically varied and visually interesting of the island's green spaces. Public access will be permitted beginning during the summer of 1982, with the first of nine scattered parking areas being completed — most likely along Gouin Boulevard — at that time. There is a parking lot at the College of St. Jean Vianney (the college, along with a religious retreat house farther west along Gouin Boulevard, will remain in existence although surrounded by the park); however, park visitors are not encouraged to use this private facility. Those who come by bus, of course, can simply get off in the vicinity of the park and select a point at which to enter.

> *PUBLIC TRANSIT: From Ile de la Visitation, walk two blocks to Henri Bourassa Boulevard and take the east-*

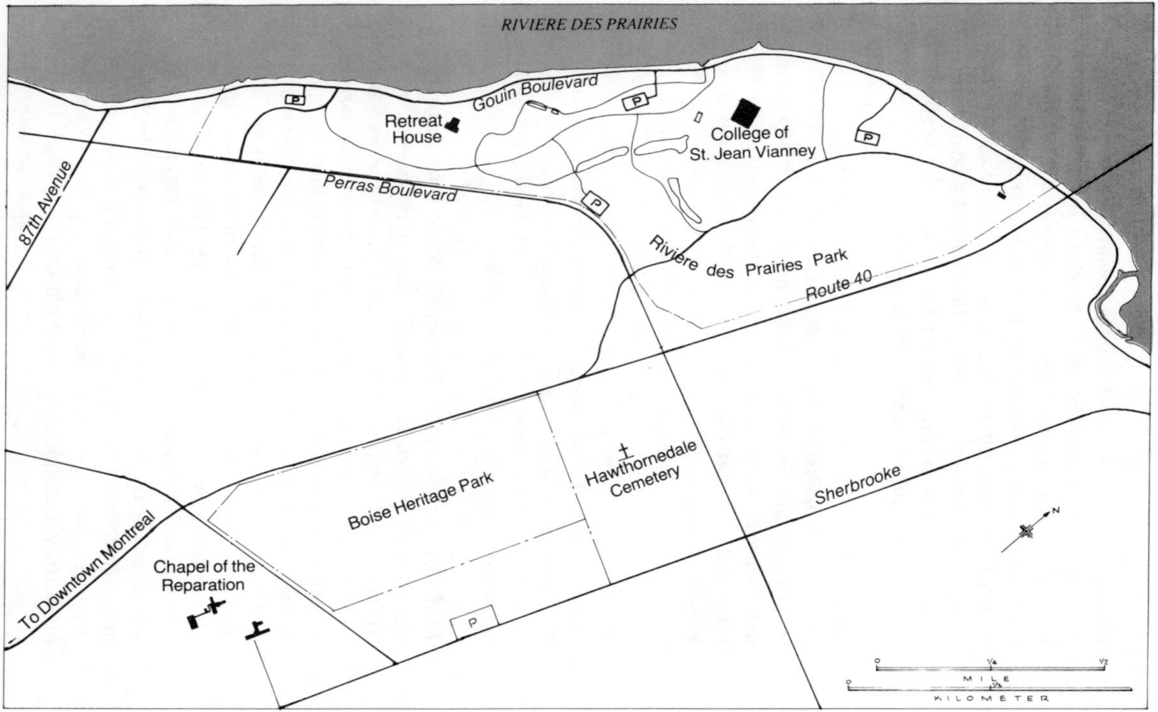
RIVIERE DES PRAIRIES
Gouin Boulevard
Retreat House
College of St. Jean Vianney
P
87th Avenue
Perras Boulevard
Riviere des Prairies Park
Route 40
Hawthornedale Cemetery
Boise Heritage Park
Sherbrooke
To Downtown Montreal
Chapel of the Reparation
N
0
1/4
1/2
MILE
KILOMETER

COUNTRY WALKS

bound Number 41 bus. At Gouin Boulevard and 87th Avenue — the end of the line — transfer to the Number 82 bus, which continues along Gouin Boulevard past the park. From downtown Montreal, take Metro Line 2 to Henri Bourassa station. The station attendant will direct you to the intersection of Henri Bourassa Boulevard and Rue St. Hubert, where the Number 41 bus route begins. Take the Number 41 and continue as above.

AUTOMOBILE: From Ile de la Visitation, simply head east on Gouin Boulevard for approximately 10 miles. The drive along the river is a pleasant one, although stop signs are frequent. After you pass the hydro lines, watch for the blue-and-white park signs. If you reach the auto route overpass (Route 40), you have passed the park.

From downtown Montreal, take Sherbrooke east to Pointe aux Trembles. Take a sharp left turn onto Gouin Boulevard (less than 1 mile beyond this point, Sherbrooke reaches the end of Montreal Island and funnels traffic onto the Legardeur Bridge). Follow Gouin Boulevard for approximately 1 mile; once you have passed beneath the auto route overpass, the park is on your left.

THE WALK: The trails to be built at Riviere des Prairies will extend throughout the park, and will accommodate walkers, cyclists, and cross-country skiers. Specially designated ski trails will likely be kept to a minimum during the park's early years, in order that patterns may be shifted to prevent compacting the soil. Eventually, most ski routes will probably follow bike paths. An advantage of this proposal will be that skiers — as well as walkers — will be able to make use of the bike route linking Riviere des Prairies with the new Boise Heritage Park, the entrance to which will be approximately 2 miles to the west (see below). Removal of skis will be necessary at the auto route overpass, but skiing along the remainder of the way should be as smooth as the snow cover allows.

ILE DE LA VISITATION

Within Riviere des Prairies, trails will weave through a mixed wooded and meadow environment, past a chain of small lakes at the center of the park. Fishing will be encouraged, and canoe rentals are a future possibility. Visitors will also be able to walk along a two-mile riverfront, also ideal for fishing and boating, and enjoy picnic areas, playing fields, and — according to current plans — a small open-air theater.

Upon leaving Riviere des Prairies, it is not possible to travel much further east on Montreal Island. Here is where the river which gives this park its name flows into the St. Lawrence. In French, this area is called *Bout de l'Ile*, the end of the island, and that is what it is. The municipality to which this extremity belongs is called Pointe aux Trembles, after the grove of aspen trees which grew here during the early days of New France. The leaves of aspens are said, in English, to "tremble"; the linguistic connection is evident. Here, in the late seventeenth century, the ubiquitous Sulpicians built a fortified mill. In 1690 and again in 1691, its walls protected settlers retreating from battles with the Iroquois.

If you drive from Riviere des Prairies to the end of Gouin Boulevard and turn right onto Sherbrooke, you will soon approach the last of these three new parks, the Boise Heritage. This is the least developed of the group, with land acquisition from the municipality of Pointe aux Trembles not yet complete and work not expected to begin until 1983. However, it has been the practice for Pointe aux Trembles to blaze ski trails (in 1980-81, a total of approximately 6 miles) within the projected park grounds, and the Urban Community of Montreal will continue this practice when the land transfer is completed. As you drive towards the city in winter, watch for the sign on the right shoulder of the road, just beyond Hawthornedale Cemetery. (As of this writing, signs have not been posted in summer.) Another nearby CUM acquisition will be the Bois de la Reparation, which surrounds the Chapel of the Reparation, a popular

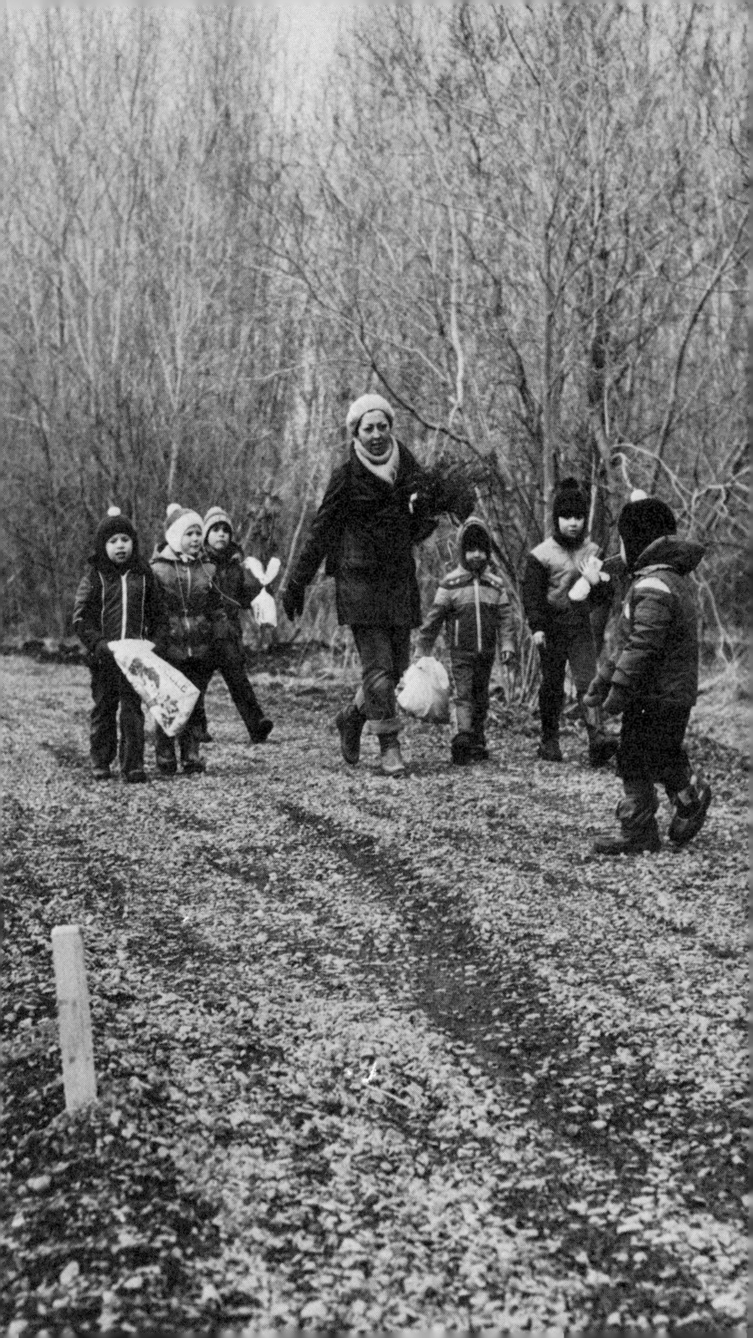

ILE DE LA VISITATION

local shrine. The same bicycle path that joins Riviere des Prairies with Boise Heritage will extend to Bois de la Reparation. It is still too early to speculate on further plans for trails and facilities within the latter two parks.

PUBLIC TRANSIT: The ride from downtown Montreal to Boise Heritage involves the Metro and two buses, and is not recommended until the park is developed further. Nor is there a direct bus connection from Riviere des Prairies.

AUTOMOBILE: From downtown Montreal, follow directions given above for Riviere des Prairies via Sherbrooke, but don't go quite as far. Look for the park on your left, just past the sign for the Chapel of the Reparation.

For information on any of the parks described in this chapter, write Communaute Urbaine de Montreal, Service de la planification du territoire, 2 Complexe Desjardins, Case postale 129, Montreal, Quebec H5B 1E6.

16

LES FORESTIERS OUTDOOR CENTER

Walking, ski touring, and snowshoeing — 10 miles of trails in a unique 1200-acre outdoor recreation and education center 30 miles west of Montreal on the peninsula which lies between the Lake of Two Mountains and the St. Lawrence River. Camping and lodge accommodations are available for overnight visitors; special attention is given to school groups.

DRIVING ALONG RUE LOTBINIERE OUEST on the last leg of a trip to Les Forestiers Outdoor Center, you begin to think that you have taken a wrong turn — not only onto the wrong road, but into the wrong environment. For the last few miles, you have been traveling through pleasant farmland; suddenly, a huge expanse of sand appears. Sand, like at the beach. You drive on, wondering about the appropriateness of the name "Les Forestiers." To make things even stranger, people are driving heavy machinery across the sand. You have stumbled, it seems, upon some vast construction project in the desert. But, a line of trees in the distance brings you back to Quebec, and a few minutes' patience brings you into their shadow and onto the grounds of the outdoor center of Les Forestiers.

Despite the fact that you have come to find out about the center, it is impossible to address your first questions to any topic but the Saharan scene through which you have just driven. But, the explanations are simple enough. The sand is a glacial deposit, and it has been lying exposed since the receding of the Champlain Sea. As for the machinery, it belongs to a school for heavy

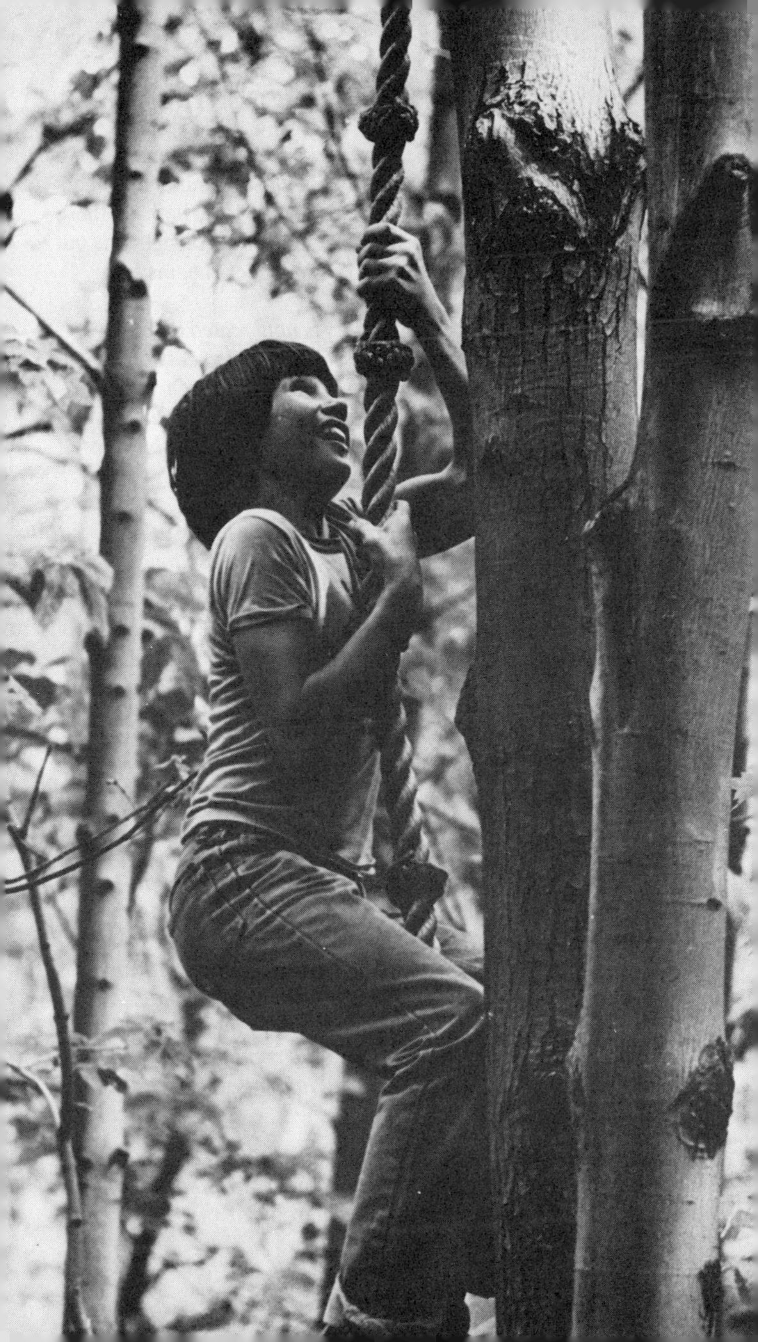

COUNTRY WALKS

equipment operators, and the drivers are trainees. There is also a sand "mine" here, which will probably close within a few years as the supply of marketable sand runs out. But, both of these incongruous neighbors are easily forgotten — out of sight and out of mind — once an exploration of Les Forestiers begins.

PUBLIC TRANSIT: Les Forestiers is not located along any main rail or bus lines, and is consequently not accessible by public transportation. Vaudreuil, which can be reached by bus or train from Montreal, is 7 miles to the east, which is too far unless the Canadian Pacific begins to allow bicycles on board.

AUTOMOBILE: Leave Montreal via Route 40 westbound. After crossing the bridge over Lake of Two Mountains, follow the signs for Route 540 south. Stay on 540 for only 1 mile, bearing right onto the exit ramp leading to Route 340. Take Route 340 westbound. After approximately 5 miles, you will come to a fork. Bear right (almost straight ahead); you are now on Rue Lotbiniere Ouest. Follow this road for approximately 1 mile until you see the sand flats. At this point the road curves left and then right again; continue through these curves, cross the sand flats, and watch for the Les Forestiers entrance on your left.

Visitors to Les Forestiers should be aware that the center is only about 15 miles from the shrine and mountain at Rigaud, described in Chapter 12. A day trip could easily include stops at both areas. To get to Rigaud from Les Forestiers, drive back along Rue Lotbiniere Ouest, turning left at the first intersection after the road rejoins Route 340. Turn left at the town of St. Lazare, and continue for 5 miles to Route 201. Turn right onto 201, and continue for 4 miles until you reach Route 342. Turn left and follow Route 342 into Rigaud.

Les Forestiers differs from the Longueuil *plein air* center described in Chapter 6, and indeed from all of the locations

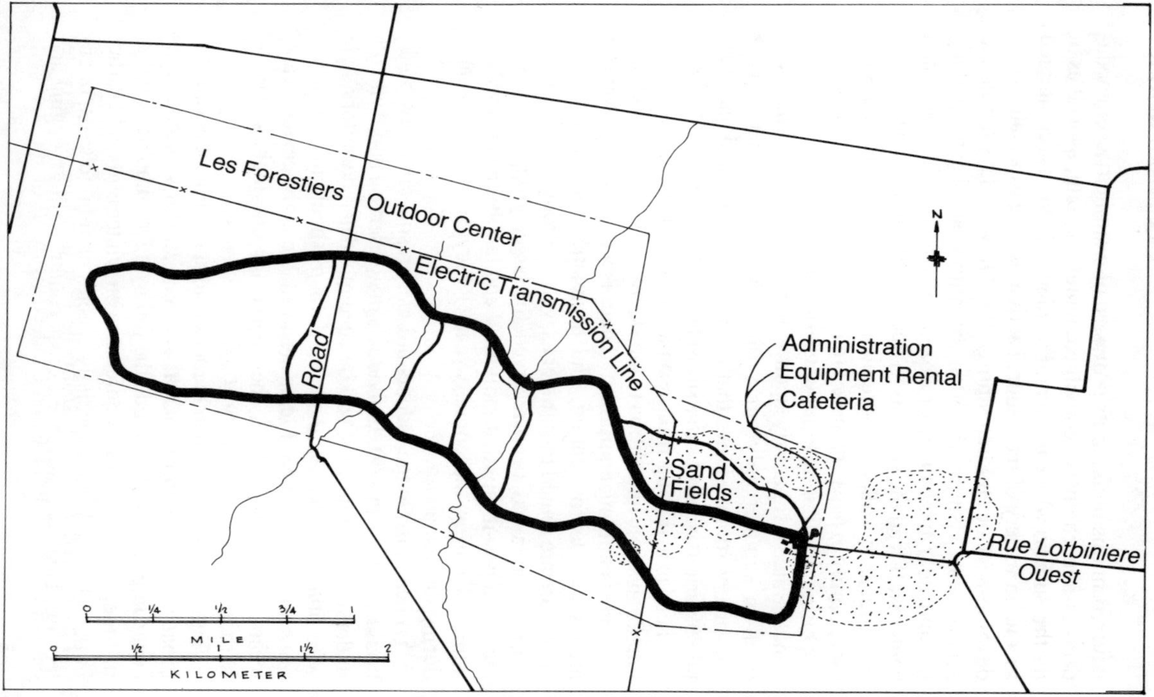
Les Forestiers
Outdoor Center
Electric Transmission Line
Road
Administration
Equipment Rental
Cafeteria
Sand
Fields
Rue Lotbiniere
Ouest
N
0
1/4
1/2
3/4
1
MILE
0
1/2
1
1½
2
KILOMETER

COUNTRY WALKS

covered in this book, in its provision of overnight accommodations and its extensive equipment rental program, as well as in the workshops which it offers. Founded in 1974, it is committed to a wide variety of recreational activities, and especially to the development of children's programs. On weekdays during the school year, visitors will often see yellow buses in the parking lot and hear the voices of dozens of children. Teachers and center staff lead the students in tree identification games, nature interpretation walks, and orientation. On weekends and in summer, family groups are more predominant.

During its first several years of operation, Les Forestiers concentrated exclusively upon winter activities, and has been open in summer only since 1981. A look into the center's equipment rooms shows that the months of ice and snow are taken seriously here: skis, snowshoes, and skates are available — there is a skating rink, a separate snowshoeing area, and a toboggan slide, in addition to the ski trails — as is an assortment of winter camping equipment. There is a one-square-kilometer area set aside for tenting, and necessities such as tents and cookware are rented in summer as well. (Through 1981, the tent camping area has been reserved for larger groups; however, there is a possibility that individual and family campers will be admitted during the coming years.) Bicycles are also rented during the summer.

You can also lodge indoors at Les Forestiers in a new bunkhouse which sleeps 60. Individuals may reserve a bunk with the understanding that they will be accommodated dormitory style with other members of their sex. Groups should make reservations well in advance. Meals are available at the center's cafeteria. As of early 1981, the charge for one night's stay — without meals — was only $6.00.

The workshops and conferences held at Les Forestiers cover a broad range of environmental and recreational subjects. A recent sampling would include the following: ornithology (3 days in June, with a separate conference on winter birds held earlier in the year); insects, especially species harmful to trees; orienteering; basic and advanced cross-country skiing; jogging and

Young pines anchor sandy soil near Les Forestiers Outdoor Center

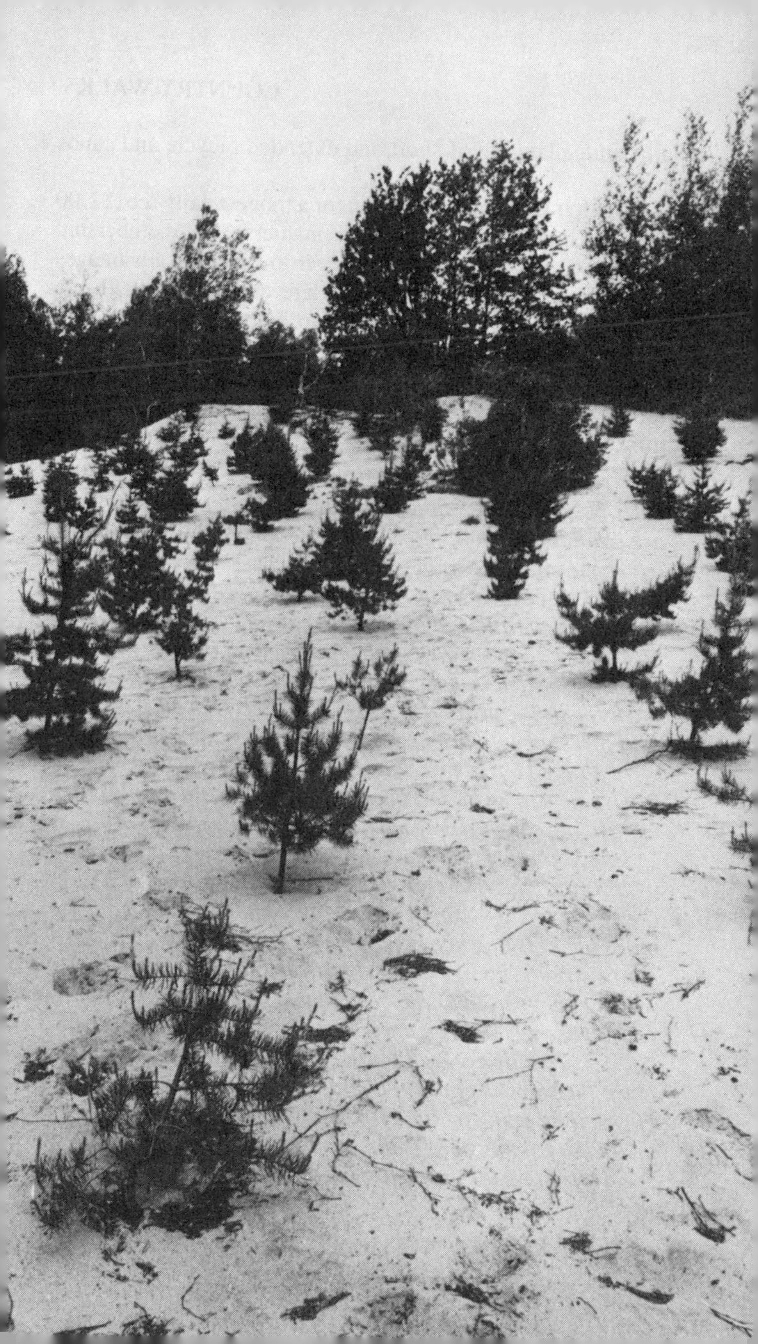

COUNTRY WALKS

health; and, planning of short and extended bicycle and canoe trips.

Although it is open to the public for a modest daily fee ($2.00 per day, winter, 1980-81), Les Forestiers is a membership organization, whose directors are eager to stress the advantages of belonging. Family memberships are available on either a seasonal or yearly basis, and entitle cardholders to participate in all conferences and workshops without charge, to attend parties and other social events at the center, and — under a plan currently being considered — to receive discounts on overnight lodging.

THE WALK: Maps of the trail network at Les Forestiers are available at the center's reception building, just to the left of the entrance road. The trails extend westward from the entrance, in the opposite direction (needless to say) of the activities which go on in that enormous natural sandbox. The trails keep largely to the periphery of the center's property, which is leased for 25 years from the adjoining towns of St. Lazare and St. Clet. The interior of the tract is well forested with birches and evergreens, some of which were planted by the provincial government forty years ago in response to farmers who complained that their fields were being covered with sand whenever windstorms arose.

Since ski tourers account for so much of Les Forestiers trail traffic, the route has been laid out in the form of a one-way circuit — approximately 3½ miles out, and 3½ miles back. But, since not all skiers prefer to make the entire circuit, there are four separate cross-link trails which may be used to shorten the trip. There are only two road crossings, one on the way out and one on the way back. The trails are well blazed in winter and summer. Once the snow is gone, of course, there are no rules concerning one-way travel, and it is enjoyable to wander up and down the cross trails, trying to identify different species among the profusion of wildflowers which grow here.

LES FORESTIERS OUTDOOR CENTER

Les Forestiers Outdoor Center, 1677 Avenue du Centre de Plein Air, Les Cedres, Quebec, is open throughout the year. For information and reservations (necessary only for overnight accommodations), call 514-452-4736.

BIBLIOGRAPHY

Beston, Henry. *The St. Lawrence*. New York and Toronto: Farrar and Rinehart, 1942. (Rivers of America Series)

Chevrier, Lionel. *The St. Lawrence Seaway*. New York: St. Martin's Press, 1959.

Geological Association of Canada and the Mineral Association of Canada. *Guidebook: Geology of Parts of Eastern Ontario and Western Quebec*. Kingston, Ontario: 1967.

Jenkins, Kathleen. *Montreal: Island City of the St. Lawrence*. Garden City, New York: Doubleday, 1966.

Lavender, David. *Winner Take All: The Trans-Canada Canoe Trail*. New York and Toronto: McGraw-Hill, 1977. (The American Trails Series)

Leclaire, Alphonse. *Guide Along the St. Lawrence*. Montreal: Sir Joshua Reynolds Art Publishing Company, 1906.

Olmsted, Frederick L. *Mount Royal, Montreal*. New York: G. P. Putnam's Sons, 1881.

Potvin, Damase. *Le Saint Laurent et Ses Isles: Histoire, Legendes, Anecdotes, Description, Topographie*. Quebec: Editions Garneau, 1945.

Tulchinsky, Gerald J. J. "The Construction of the First Lachine Canal, 1815-1826." Unpublished thesis, McGill University, 1960.

ABOUT THE AMC

The Appalachian Mountain Club is a non-profit volunteer organization of over 25,000 members. Centered in the northeastern United States with headquarters in Boston, its membership is worldwide. The AMC was founded in 1876, making it the oldest and largest organization of its kind in America. Its existence has been committed to conserving, developing, and managing dispersed outdoor recreational opportunities for the public in the Northeast and its efforts in the past have endowed it with a significant public trust and its volunteers and staff today maintain that tradition.

Ten regional chapters from Maine to Pennsylvania, some sixty committees, and hundreds of volunteers supported by a dedicated professional staff join in administering the Club's wide-ranging programs. Besides volunteer organized and led expeditions, these include research, backcountry management, trail and shelter construction and maintenance, conservation, and outdoor education. The Club operates a unique system of eight alpine huts in the White Mountains, a base camp and public information center at Pinkham Notch, New Hampshire, a new public service facility in the Catskill Mountains of New York, five full service camps, four self-service camps, and nine campgrounds, all open to the public. Its Boston headquarters houses not only a public information center but also the largest mountaineering library and research facility in the U. S. The Club also conducts leadership workshops, mountain search and rescue, and a youth opportunity program for disadvantaged urban young people. The AMC publishes guidebooks, maps, and America's oldest mountaineering journal, *Appalachia*.

We invite you to join and share in the benefits of membership. Membership brings a subscription to the monthly bulletin *Appalachia*; discounts on publications and at the huts and camps managed by the Club; notices of trips and programs; and, association with chapters and their meetings and activities. Most important, membership offers the opportunity to support and share in the major public service efforts of the Club.

Membership is open to the general public upon completion of an application form and payment of an initiation fee and annual dues. Information on membership as well as the names and addresses of the secretaries of local chapters may be obtained by writing to: The Appalachian Mountain Club, 5 Joy Street, Boston, Massachusetts 02108, or calling during business hours 617-523-0636.